The Devil's Advocate's Guide
to
PLANNING YOUR BUSINESS WEBSITE

Elaine Meszaros

Cover design and logo by Elaine Meszaros, EMGraphics LLC.
Cover photo Agony of Cain
© Maria Egupova | Dreamstime.com

Meszaros, Elaine
The Devil's Advocate's Guide to Planning Your Website
ISBN-13: 978-0996354301
ISBN-10: 0996354301

1. Non-fiction. 2. Computers & Technology. 3.Web Development &
Design. 4.Web Design.

EMGraphics, LLC
emgraphics.net

Many thanks to Ruth Meszaros, CJ Kucera and Dr. Andrew Ruis
for their eagle-eyed proofreading and editing.
Without you, so many of my typos would be going virile.

Table of Contents

Devil's Advocate

noun

"A person who advocates an opposing or unpopular cause for the sake of argument or to expose it to a thorough examination."

- Dictionary.com

I call myself "the Devil's Advocate" as this is a role I often find myself playing with potential clients. One of the first things I often get asked is, "How much is a website?" To which I answer, "Well, how much is a car? Are we talking a third-hand AMC Gremlin that spews exhaust and smells funky? Or are we talking a brand-new BMW with seat-warmers and special bucket-sized drink holders?" I then go on to ask a lot of detailed questions, very few of which they can answer.

Not planning before starting to build a website can be extremely costly, time-consuming and wildly frustrating.

Let's say:

- You need your online orders to be shipped in parts, but the new cart that is half done doesn't support this option. Do you scrap it and start again, or pay for expensive custom coding?
- You bought a domain 5 years ago, but since you didn't renew it there is now a placeholder saying it is available for the low, low price of $700. It's a shame you printed all those brochures with it already...
- The new website is almost ready to launch when someone points out that the colors and fonts are identical to your main competitor's website. "Sincerest form of flattery" aside, you don't

want them (or your potential customers) to think you were just copying the competition.

All of these problems could have been solved with some simple planning, but now they will cost a great deal to fix.

A website isn't an object you can purchase. It is something you create through a series of steps and processes.

There are hundreds, if not thousands, of books and articles available exhorting the joys of creating a website and how it will drive business to you in droves. All you need is happy thoughts and it will be nothing but rainbows, sunshine and rivers of cash. The reality is: a businesses that has a plan (and often a back-up plan) will be infinitely more successful than one winging it on wishful thinking. Simply assuming that all will be well is naïve at best, dangerous and counter-productive at worst.

For many, a website is just a thing you have when you own a business. Often it is an after-thought, popped together at the last minute. Other times it is a chore dumped on an assistant or intern. This is a strange attitude, as a website is often your most viewed piece of advertising. It is your public face to the world—available 24/7 to anyone, anywhere. The cost per view is infinitesimal, unlike print media which can cost cents to dollars per piece. Your website can sell products, gather leads, offer support, provide information and persuade new customers to try your product or service *all the time*. It never closes.

While much of this book consists of practical advice on what to do, it also poses a number of open-ended questions. This is **your** business and **your** website. An outsider can't tell you what how your business works or what is best for you. **You** need to know the answers to these questions. And if you don't know the the answers currently, *find out*.

2

Whether the knowledge applies to your website or not, it is all good to know. Tailor your website to your market, provide useful content and make it attractive and easy to use. Take the time to plan your website and it will be much more successful and useful. Plus, the creation process will be far less painful.

—

I've included some anecdotes about funny, clever and occasionally mind-boggling things clients have done throughout the years. On the whole, the vast majority of the clients are pleasantly and delightfully normal. We talk about what they want, I write up a proposal, they agree, I do the work, we tweak things a bit and it goes live. But once in awhile I come across a doozy. Let them be life lessons.

—

Chapter 1
Why Are You Building a Website?

When I ask a new client why they want a site, I sometimes get remarkably vague answers. "My brother-in-law said I should have one," or, "Well, everyone else has one..."

The main reason most people want a website is to **market their business or product and increase sales.** It's really nothing more complex than this.

The function of your website is to compel other people to take some sort of **action**. You may want visitors to buy a product, sign up for a newsletter, read your posts, visit a physical location or a combination of all of these. To get people to take action, you need to present them with an argument for *why* they should take action, and a way for them to do so. Make it easy for your visitors to take action.

What do you want people to do on your website?
- Buy a product.
- Get directions or hours to visit a physical location.
- Sign up for a newsletter or mailing list.
- Read information on products or services.
- Give you their contact information.
- Share information about your website with others.
- Download forms or documents.
- Submit applications or forms.
- Comment on website content or add suggestions.

By convincing the visitor to take an action, you are encouraging them to provide revenue to your company - either through a direct sale or by providing more information on your products or services.

Ask yourself, **"What sort of information or content can I offload to the website to save me time?"** Most businesses spend an inordinate amount of time answering the same questions and providing the same basic information over and over. Much of this information can be posted on the site, cutting down greatly on repetitive time-wasters.

This can include:

- Standard information about the company's services or products offered.
- Maps, directions and hours.
- Upcoming events.
- How to purchase products online or elsewhere.
- Sales and specials.
- Contact information.
- Social media links.
- Job postings and applications.
- Email lists.

The website should be tailored to appeal to your audience and make it easier and more pleasant for visitors to do business with your company.

Additionally, the website should work FOR you to save you time, money and hassle. Plan ways for your website to assist you and make your job easier.

I had a company contact me to do some search engine optimization (SEO) on their site, as they weren't making any sales. I pointed out that their retail system was far too complex.

They required anyone who wanted to shop online first to fill out a contact form with name, address, phone and email. An employee would hand-approve the application (double-checking to make sure the applicant wasn't a corporate spy!), then send them a password. When the applicant got their password, they were finally allowed to enter the shop and see prices.

For cheese. In Wisconsin.

—

Chapter 2
What is Your Website's Target Audience?

Who do you want to use your website? What is your target audience? "Anyone and everyone!" you may say. (Well, probably not the Amish.) This is not true. Yes, there are certainly sites that target nearly everyone, such as amazon.com, but even in those cases there are certain visitors who are higher-priority targets.

You need to identify a sufficiently constrained audience to create a website that will appeal and be useful to that audience. Clearly defining your core demographic can make tailoring your website's content, design and functionality infinitely easier.

Consider:
- What economic class are you targeting? A website for a luxury market is far different from one which focuses on bargains.
- Are your products or services a spontaneous purchase or things customers will consider carefully?
- Do you have a product or service that will only serve a certain geographic location or community? For instance, a retirement community does not need to target the teen market.
- Are you more interested in selling online or getting people through the door of a brick-and-mortar establishment?
- Are you interested in selling directly to the retail market or wholesaling business to business?

What demographic groups do your potential target markets include? The major ones include:

Age of Visitors: What is the age of the visitors who may use your website? A website targeting teens will be different from one targeting retirees.

Gender: Is your website tailored for one gender? Conversely, do you want to make sure that all people feel welcome?

Ethnicity: Do you expect any particular ethnic groups to use your website? How can you tailor the website to cater to them? For instance, would a Spanish-language version of the website be useful?

Geographic location: Are your visitors more likely to be in a big city or rural area?

Disability: Will your users need special features to help them navigate the website? For instance, offer the ability to enlarge the font for users with vision impairments or add audio or visual descriptions of products.

Mobility: Will your visitors use your website because they are home-bound or geographically isolated? Conversely, is your website there to encourage them to visit a physical location?

Income level: What economic groups do you think will use your website? A website catering to low-income visitors looking for deals will have a far different focus than one selling luxury goods. Of course, you can offer varying levels to appeal to a broader range of potential customers.

Organization type: While many sites are tailored for the retail shopper, other sites are tailored for wholesaling, business-to-business services, non-profit institutions, or government agencies.

You can't be all things to all people.

Differentiate Yourself

As the preceding sections suggest, a key element of a successful website is differentiation. Your website needs to differentiate your business from your competitors.

You can differentiate yourself by:
- Offering a unique product or service.
- Offering products or services at special times - *weekend or evening hours.*
- Offering high-quality service and extras - *free loaner cars.*

- Offering free shipping or a free gift with a purchase. *"Free" can be a relative term, as the cost is often rolled into some other part of the price.*
- Offering discounts for regulars – *coupon codes, discount cards, customer-only surprise previews and sales.*
- Sending reminders – *email reminders of a hair appointment.*
- Offering expedited shipping (at no extra cost) on all orders.
- Having a unique or convenient location - *the only liposuction clinic attached to a Chinese buffet!*
- Having the lowest prices available.
- Being the only provider of this service or product – *fine art, specialized parts, Consulting Wizard.*
- Having unique product sizing – *plus-size clothing, fabric by the 1/4 yard, single LEDs, bulk cases of goods.*
- Offering warrantees or guarantees of quality and service.

If you have a warrantee or guarantee on products or services, **you must honor what you promise.** Word-of-mouth is a great way to build your business but it can just as easily sink it. One bad review on Google, Yelp, Angie's List or Urban Spoon can do more damage than a slew of good reviews.

Be honest. People would much rather be told the truth than be lied to and have false expectations. A false promise of delivery "tomorrow, for sure!" is far more damaging than a truthful "Friday at the earliest."

Use common sense:

- Don't sell products you know are shoddy or dangerous.
- Don't promise what you can't deliver.
- Don't offer services that you can't perform.
- Don't offer what you don't stock.
- Do honor any specials or coupons you have announced.

Create an Ideal Customer

Mentally create an ideal customer or customers. Then tailor your website to them. Let's say you sell high-quality clothing for professional women. Your ideal customers may be:

Professional women with disposable income but little time: doctors or lawyers, perhaps. These women want to buy a couple of complete outfits at once.

Professional women with lower incomes: teachers or librarians, say. They may want a few basic items to add to their wardrobes. These women will wait for a sale and not care about the season.

Women looking for a bit of a pick-me-up or recreational shoppers. They may have extensive wardrobes or very small ones. These women may be more interested in accessories or show-stopping pieces like scarves, socks or jewelry to perk up what they have. They shop on a whim, just for fun or to find cheap(er) items.

You now have three groups here and can focus on them in different ways. You can also discount other groups – such as men, teens and dogs. Sure, you may get occasional shoppers from outside your target demographic, but it doesn't pay to cater to them.

Plan how your website will entice and retain each of these groups.

The women with **disposable income** will want to see the collections early, even before they are widely available (in stores). You need to give them a way to see the items and pre-order them. To market to them, you may offer discounts if they buy an entire outfit at once. You could guarantee that they will receive their order before the looks are available in the shop, or promise that their size will be in stock.

For **women with lower incomes,** advertise a sale or offer coupons for end-of-season pieces. Perhaps offer them a free item like a scarf with a purchase of two or more sweaters. They may have intended only to buy one, but it is hard to pass up a good deal on a useful and high-quality item when it comes with a freebie! Not only that, you won't be left with as many left over pieces to mark down further or return.

Finally, the **random buyers** may also appreciate random sales. Send out email blasts for one-day sales on bracelets or have surprise discounts on funky socks. This will keep them coming back, either to the website or via marketing material, so they don't miss a flash-special.

As you design the site, keep referring to these ideal customers in your head. Imagine what they will be most interested in while they are on your website. Remember, this is *your* business, but the website is for *them*. It should be built to appeal to the customers, not you and your staff.

Somewhere out there is a buyer for anything, but you need more than one person to create a feasible business.

Be Realistic About the Market

Be realistic about who is going to be buying your products or services. You may have pitched the idea to a best friend or family members and had a strong, enthusiastic response. Your mom may tell you she loves it. But does this reflect the reality of the actual marketplace?
- Is there demand for the product or service?
- What sort of competition is already out there doing something similar? If so, how well are they doing? Do they have positive or negative reviews online? Have you heard positive or negative things about them? **Can you do better?**
- Is there a large enough market?

- Have non-family/friends shown interest in your idea?
- Have you done some market research on your products/services, your target audience, locations and more?
- Have you spoken to someone from SCORE? The Service Corp of Retired Executives (score.org) will match up you up with a professional who will give you free advice.
- Do you have a wide enough range of products or services to sustain you in the current economy?
- Do you have a business plan, with back-up contingencies?
- Will your products or services be sustainable in a downturn?
- How dependent will this business be on another company, such as a wholesale supplier?

—

One of my clients started a side business. The wholesaler failed to fulfill his orders and disappeared. My client lost his side business, his main business that was on the same business loan, and his house. I got off easy (I was making the wholesaler's site) and only got screwed out of $700.

—

You are not selling items or services, you are selling the alleviation of a problem.

Solve Your Customers' Problems

No one goes out to buy a bottle of oven cleaner because they've always wanted to own one and can't wait to cradle it in their arms, lovingly stroking the label. No, they want to clean their oven more easily. No one hires an accountant because they want a big pile of paperwork and to give the government a bunch of money. They hire the accountant to alleviate the anxiety and stress of doing complex math and the paperwork themselves. You don't build a deck on your house because you think it needs some wood bits sticking out of the side. You want to socialize with friends and neighbors. Making friends, grilling in nice weather and feeling happy has nothing to do with a pile of two-by-fours.

Include text on your site telling your potential customers how you will solve their problems. Once established, include reviews and testimonials from happy customers.

Chapter 3
What Content Should Be on Your Website?

There are essentially two types of information on a website - **standard content** and **differentiating features.**

Standard Content

The **standard content** has evolved over the years to become the core of any website and now is expected by users.

This includes:

- The company name and logo at the top of the page.
- Homepage text giving an overview of what the website is about.
- Contact information - email, phone and possibly an address in the header or footer. The contact information should also be on its own page.
- An "About" page describing the company and employees, some history and other background information.
- Uniform links on all pages, including a link back to the homepage.
- Uniform design or designs to indicate that all the pages are on the same website.

Not sticking to the standards will not only confuse your users but may also make you look unprofessional, uncaring or lazy. Ignore these rules at your peril.

Years ago I saw a beautiful website that was based on tropical flowers. However, there were no words to indicate which link went where. You had to guess that the picture of the Bird of

Paradise went to Contact, the Hibiscus was About Us, etc. The website was totally redesigned within a few months.

Users expect to load a page and find the **name of the website** in the **top header,** and often a logo. This indicates that they are indeed on the correct page. After all, there can be more than one company with the same name. Including a name, logo and tagline assures the visitor that they are at the correct site.

The **homepage** should always contain at least one paragraph of text. While there is often the temptation to have a big splash page or animation, you aren't doing yourself any favors. Search engines (such as Google) place the most emphasis on written (text) content. If you only have a large video or flash animation running on your homepage, there are no words available for the search engine to categorize the page. While you can and should have ALT tags—hidden tags that describe an image or animation—these are a poor substitute for real text. Often they are just a vague description of the image: "XYZ company animation." You certainly can have an awesome, eye-popping visual opening, but do have a block of text below it.

What should this homepage text include? **Who** you are, **what** you do/sell, **where you are** located, **why** you do this (differentiate), and **how** you want your users to react.

For instance:

XYZ Corp. is a leader is heat-resistant widgets in North America. With locations in all 50 states, Canada and Mexico, we provide more than 10 million units a year to 2,000 locations. Our patented UL approved widgets are preferred two to one over other brands. They are used by everyone from local contractors to the builders of skyscrapers. We aim to provide the best product possible and are continually innovating. Find a retailer in your area, order wholesale online, find a spec sheet or contact our knowledgeable staff through our chat service.

Services or Items for Sale - Whether you are selling online or not, you need to describe what services or products you sell. What is it that you offer to make your income?

Contact information - There aren't any hard and fast rules for contact information placement. Since this is often some of the most important information on the site, a bit of duplication is fine. You may want your contact information – email, phone, address – in the header, footer, or sidebar and then have an additional link directly to a page. This will ensure it can be found, regardless of the user's expectation.

If you are a solely online presence (no physical store), you are under no obligation to post your address or even a phone number. Do make sure your email is functioning and consider adding something like a chat feature or twitter support feed.

A **contact form** is a great way to both filter out the spam/junk comments and to get a better idea of what a potential customer wants. They can indicate areas of interest, indicate they want to be added to a list, send questions and request specific information. Also, a form can hide your email address, which cuts down on some spam.

Links to the sub-pages on a website (any page other than the homepage) should also be in a standard position – the header or a sidebar. Links on the bottom/footer are hard to find, as they often are "below the fold"– this is a holdover term from printing where the most important news stories are at the top of a newspaper, above the center fold of the paper. Links should remain in the same locations throughout the website. Users will quickly become used to a link being in a certain spot. If the order changes, they will become frustrated.

If your website is large, you can have more than one link menu. Perhaps you want your main topics in the top menu, then current blog posts or featured products and cart in a sidebar. Breaking up lots of links into separate menus can make the website more compact and easier to navigate.

Additionally, **drop-down menus** are a great way to offer access to areas of information on the website. They can drop-down from a link, fly out to the side, or open like an accordion. You can even have sub-sub-menus!

Users expect a **link back to the homepage.** This may seem counter-intuitive since most users enter the page via the homepage. However, many users still feel compelled to go back to the homepage after visiting sub-pages, either to leave the website or perhaps to see if they missed additional information.

Your **About** information should include a description of the company and its history, provide information on the owner and any employees, and indicate the professional background, skills and experience of the personnel. The key is to make this information interesting, brief and pertinent. You want to create a personal rapport with future customers and also prove your bona fides. By providing some personal information and history, you assure readers that you and your company have the products, skills or experience they need.

Add information such as:
- What skills and experience do the owners or employees have that relate to the business?

- What education or training do the owners or employees have? A short CV/resume is often a good addition for more dense personal history.
- How many years have you been in business?
- A company history, particularly if the firm is established. Old pictures are a great addition, too.
- If this is a new venture, what previous experience do you have at other companies or in a related field?
- Have you: won any special awards, received patents, been honored in any way or have a special certification?
- Have articles or interviews been published about your company?

What Makes You Different and Special?

The differentiating **text and features** are what make you stand out. You should already know what differentiates your business. Now you need to say it and show it with a clear argument to describe why the visitor should use your services or purchase your product.

Some content and features you can add to stand out:
- Customer testimonials.
- Good reviews and press.
- Descriptions of speciality or unique services or goods you provide.
- Descriptions of special, unique or advanced training that you have.
- Special hours or locations, such as late evening hours or house calls.

You can also add **special features** to your website to help make the website more useful and interesting to users. You don't just want them interested in your product or service, you want them to come back again and again and to recommend the website to their friends.

While some companies become starry eyed over the idea of an app or fancy animation, users will be just as appreciative of a few special, useful touches.

For instance:
- Adding a calendar of local events you will participate in, workshops/seminars you will host, upcoming sales and more.
- In-depth information on products, like material handling sheets or washing instructions.
- Tips and tricks on upkeep or repair for a product.
- Fun facts related to your product or service.
- Listings and maps of retailers that carry your products.
- Directions and maps, plus parking or bus route information.
- Suggested reading, links to related articles or a blog of your own writing.
- *Interesting* personal stories on how you started your company or its history.
- Calculation and estimate tools or forms, such as a square footage or mortgage calculator.
- Charts and graphs, such as suggested planting times for bulbs.
- Recipes that include your products.
- Photo galleries with customers using your products or at a company-sponsored event.
- Contests and photo/story submissions from happy clients.
- Directions for use or assembly.
- Where to get replacement parts and refills.
- A sign-up option for reminders, such as appointments, renewals or replacements.
- Coupons, discounts and other special sales.
- Any or all of the above sent monthly in a newsletter.

Legalities

Remember, you are ultimately responsible for your website's content. Make sure you know all the rules governing your business's website.

- Does your content need to be approved by a legal team?
- Are there legal footers, such as financial disclosures, that you need to include on every page?
- Do you need to include certain logos, such as FDIC or HUD?
- Are the offers and claims you assert on your page legally allowed by federal agencies like the ATF, FDIC, SEC and others?
- Do you need to include your accreditation or license numbers on your website?

What *Not* to Include in Your Website

**If it comes down to you asking, "Should I say this?"
then no, don't.**

Unless it *directly* pertains to your business, there are some topics that you simply should not mention on your website at all. Religion, sex and politics have no place on a business website. The purpose of a business is to make money. Even being "pro" something can seem like a coded message that certain people's business is not wanted. Alienating part of your clientele will lose you business and money. It's as simple as that.

Writing Your Content

Writing your web content is a whole book unto itself. If you are not confident with your writing skills and have the budget, a professional copy-writer can take your jottings and turn them into solid content. Otherwise, here are some tips to marshall your thoughts and create interesting, cohesive and persuasive text:

- **Write down the salient points**, add some adjectives (descriptive words) around them, then make this content into sentences by adding some verbs (action words). For instance, you may have "workshops" and "speak professionally." Expand this list into "teach small workshops at colleges and universities" and "speak to rotary clubs and schools about writing creative fiction." This becomes "I teach small workshops of ten students or fewer at colleges and universities. I can also be hired to speak to groups like rotary clubs and schools on how to write creative and engaging fiction."
- **Don't use hyperbole or make exaggerated claims.** Saying you are "the best" just begs the reader to ask "Best based on what or according to whom?" You can, and should, brag a bit when you have something to be proud of *(Midwesterners, I'm looking at you)*. Make sure your assertions are based on fact. "Everyone loves our restaurant," is hyperbole. "Voted Madison's favorite restaurant 5 years in a row by *Madison Magazine* readers," speaks to your quality and backs it up with verifiable facts.
- **Don't knock the competition.** It's tasteless and obnoxious. Think of a particularly ugly battle between politicians. Embarrassing, immature, irritating and vulgar, yes? If you insist on conveying your superiority over a competitor, stick to facts. You don't need to insult your competitor by saying, "They're never open when you need them." Instead, you can say "We're open later than anyone in town."
- **Don't write nasty things that can be actionable.** You may find yourself in court trying to defend yourself against libel.
- **Don't lie.** Besides not being ethical, the internet has an infinite memory. When you lie, you are opening yourself up to scrutiny of everything you say and do. Not only is this highly unethical, but anyone can verify in minutes whether or not your claims are true. If you do find an unintentional falsehood on your part,

admit the mistake and apologize. Trying to hide a mistake will only make it look more suspicious.

- **Explain, give details, but don't bore.** Be succinct with a description and give the major facts. If readers want more information, you can provide additional links, material data sheets, or white papers. Or have them contact you directly. You can certainly reiterate major points on different pages, but don't keep saying the same things over and over. Summarize, expand a bit and move on.

- **Keep your text blocks short.** The internet, for better or worse, has trained us to expect shorter chunks of text. We want the information and we want it fast. Scrolling through a long page of text can seem overwhelming. You can certainly write fulsome text, but make sure that text is broken up into pages with "read more" links or give a summary before a large block of content.

- **Proofread, spell-check and grammar-check your text** a few times. Have a few other people read it through, too. Often they catch mistakes you have seen so often you don't register them anymore. Or you may want to hire someone to proofread your copy. This is cheaper than having someone write all your text but still ensures a professional has looked it over. Nothing will distract a reader's eye more than a typo—for instance, "their" instead of "they're."

—

I know this from first-hand experience. I almost sent a brochure off to press extolling the virtues of our local "pubic parks."

—

Tip: If someone else is adding content to your website, the text should be submitted in a standard document format (.doc, .docx, .rtf, .txt, .pdf) or emailed. Don't use proprietary products like Publisher, Pages, QuarkXPress or other obsolete or obscure programs.

22

What Sort of Images Should I Use?

Images on a website can make or break you. You may have every feature desired, great reviews and wonderful turnaround. But if the pictures make your products look like junk, you're not going to be making a sale. No one wants to visit a store that looks dilapidated and seedy. Nor do they want to hire someone whose head shot makes them look like a serial killer in a windstorm.

A few quality images are far better than lots of crummy ones. A professional group shot of your staff is far preferable to a confusing mix of professional shots, camera phone shots and scrounged-up vacation pictures for each staff member.

What Format Should My Images Be?

Ideally you will start out with high-resolution pictures and then reduce them to 72dpi for the web. They should be saved in a format that browsers can read - JPG, GIF, PNG and increasingly SVG.

What does this mean? The **resolution** of an images indicates how much information is contained in the image. A higher resolution image has more dpi – dots (or pixels) per inch. Imagine a glossy head shot printed on photo paper next to that same image printed in a newspaper. The real photo looks great no matter how close you look at it. The newspaper photo will start breaking up into little dots of color as you bring it closer to your eye. A 72dpi image has 72 pixels across one inch. This is like the newspaper image. A high-resolution picture of 300 dpi would have 300 pixels across. (Images can go up into the thousands of dpi for resolution, but 300dpi is usually good for print.) If you were to put both of these images on a photocopier and enlarge them 200%, the photo on the photo paper would still look pretty good, though a tiny bit fuzzy. The newspaper image would be a mess; you can clearly see each ink dot that makes up the image.

A high-resolution image can be reduced in size and quality. A low-resolution image cannot be made better. It will just get blurrier and nastier looking the larger you make it. So starting with good images and reducing them is key. If you are working with a designer or shooting your own images, you may be tempted to send or take the images at a low-resolution. Don't. Stick with high-resolution images and reduce. You never know when you want to use just a part of an image, enlarge it or even use it for print, which requires high-resolution images.

Giving a designer a low-resolution photo or logo and asking them to make it larger/better is like giving a chef a cookie and saying "Find the recipe for this." They may come up with something close, but it will take A LOT of time and work. It may be close, but it won't be exact, either.

Note: Slapping a high-resolution image into your website will not give you a sharper image. It will instead enlarge the image. A 150dpi image will appear twice as large as a 72dpi image. A 300dpi image will appear four times as large as a 72dpi. Not what you intended, is it? High-resolution images will also take a great deal longer to load.

You also need to make sure the images are saved in the correct format for the web. The big three are JPG (pronounced jay-peg), GIF (jiff, like the peanut butter) or PNG (PING!). SVG is also starting to be recognized by some browsers, but not enough that you should be using it much yet. Each of these formats have different uses. JPG is the most common and gives you really nice images with lots of color yet keeps the size small. However, JPGs can't be made transparent (where you see part of the background through areas of the image). GIFs are very small and do transparency very nicely but can only have up to 256 colors. PNGs can also do transparency and become semi-opaque, so the background can be seen through the image. However, PNGs tend to be larger and take longer to load. Most sites use a mix of image formats.

If you are planning on editing photos yourself, I'd recommend snagging a copy of GIMP, a free open-source photo editing program (gimp.org). There are lots of training videos on YouTube and lynda.com. Photo editing and manipulation is a complicated subject. On the whole though, you will probably just need to resize, crop and save. If you are using a content management system like WordPress, you can do some editing directly in the program!

What Options Are There for Including Images?

Not using any images. If you don't need to directly illustrate something (like a product), you don't actually have to use any photos. Of course, the overall page design should be strong and attractive to make up for the lack of images, but it is done all the time. Clean, minimalist design with strong visual elements like colorful links, interesting fonts, icons and textures can be classic and extremely attractive.

Use stock photography or clip art. There are hundreds of places to find good free or low-priced art. If you are using a designer, they often have a huge cache of stock photography that they can add for free or low cost. The key, of course, is to make the art applicable. While nature photos have brightened many a bland page, they may not necessarily make sense on a machine fabricating website.

There are tons of places to find sets of icons and other bits of art. A vintage image here or there can be a really fun addition to the site, if it makes sense in context. Don't just add images to fill space. Nor should you mix styles (vintage here, cartoons there).

There are also dozens of places to find free stock photos. Search for "free stock photos creative commons" or "free stock photos -royalty." The creative commons license may allow you to use images (and other content) any way you'd like. Be aware that "free" and "royalty free" are two very different beasts. Free images you can use any way you wish. *Royalty-*free images mean you don't have to pay royalties based on how often they are used, but you still need to buy them.

Hire a photographer. Hiring a pro gives you a much better chance of getting clear, professional, and high-resolution images.

- Choose a photographer who specializes in the type of photos you need. Some focus on product shots, others do portraits, and plenty of studios do a mix. However, asking a friend who is primarily a wedding photographer to do product shots may not be the best choice, even if you are getting a good deal.
- Make sure you take a look at a portfolio to make sure you like the quality and style of their work. Don't hire anyone who can't show you any samples!
- Before you sign anything, be sure you have told the photographer your expectations, the parameters of the job and what the photos will be used for.
- Be sure to discuss where the images will be taken. Will you bring your products to their studio to be shot? Will they come to your office for your employee group shot?
- Make sure you understand all the costs. What is the fee for taking the photos? What is the fee for a disc of images or access to the high-resolution files? Do you also want prints? Are there package deals? Do you get actual prints or only digital files?
- Be sure you are clear on access to and ownership of the digital files. Can you use them in print? Will you get them on disk or download them from a website? How long will the download links be available? Will they include retouching and cropping?

While you may want to use the images only on the website now, in six months you may want to create a print brochure or another piece and use these images. So, do make sure the images are high-resolution for print and that there aren't any strings attached to using them elsewhere in the future.

- Have the products or people you need to be photographed ready to go. Don't waste the photographer's time (and your money) by having them wait around while you round up your staff or run around looking for products.
- Make a list of shots and angles that you will need taken. For instance, "Front, side and top of each product, along with close-up details of these areas..."

Contact the wholesale company for images. Often wholesalers will be happy to provide a retail location with professional, high-resolution images of products. They want to make sales, and ensuring that the retailers carrying their products have good images goes a long way toward that goal. Contact them and ask if they provide images or a media kit for you to use.

A note about copyright: With any of these options, make sure you understand what rights you have to use the images. Stock photo vendors will tell you clearly under what conditions you can use the images. A photographer should provide you with a contract and may want photo credit on your website. Images provided by a wholesaler may also include some stipulations, like not using them alongside their competitor's products. As tempting as it is, *never* steal images off the internet. There are lots of ways you can be found out and there are so many low-cost and free ways to get images, it simply isn't worth the hassle.

Take Your Own Photos: Of course, you can always take your own photos and not worry about any copyright issues. I've had excellent photos taken by clients and also horrible, dark, blurry images that were useless. So be realistic about your skills and your gear.

**If you take dark, low-resolution images on a cheap cell phone, they will end up looking like...
dark, low-resolution images taken on a cheap cell phone.**

At the very least, use a newer smartphone or digital camera to get clear, high-resolution images. Otherwise, ask around to see if you can borrow a camera or have a friend take the images, perhaps for an in-kind trade.

—

One of my very first freelance jobs was creating some fishing ads for my home county's tourism department. The pictures they sent me to work with were scans of polaroids from the wall of the bait shop, complete with thumb prints, fade lines from the sun, tack holes and gobs of lint and dust.

—

There are plenty of good books, short courses and websites out there on taking nice photos, but here are a few basic tips for low-tech, quick and cheap photos:
- Make sure you have strong, diffuse light. This means a couple of good light sources, not too close to the subject. Avoid glare, harsh and stark lighting (which washes out details) and deep shadows.
- Make sure your lens is clean!
- Use a tripod and shoot straight on. Avoid head shots where the subject is looking down at the camera or product pictures taken at odd angles.
- That pink thing hovering in the corner of all your shots? That's your thumb.

- Make sure your image is focused. Blurry images are very unprofessional. Take a bunch to be sure. Remember, a tripod is your friend!
- Find a plain background for your images. Busy details like patterned wallpaper are distracting.
- If you are shooting smaller products, set up a "photo booth." Use a freshly ironed sheet or clean drop-cloth as a backdrop, or paint the inside of a box matte black.
- If you are taking employee head shots, give employees adequate notice so they can make sure they are wearing nice clothing, have their hair and make-up done, and are nicely dressed. You want your employees to look friendly, relaxed, professional and accessible. No tank-tops, no crocs, no hats that hide faces, no tasteless t-shirts and no spinach in the teeth, please!
- If you would like to include a photo of your business location, be sure to pick a nice sunny day with leaves on the trees and grass on the ground. Avoid shots where there are mounds of dirty slush, the building needs a paint job or cars are blocking the view. Try to shoot from a distance, so you aren't looking up at the building, distorting its shape.
- Remember to shoot using a high-resolution setting. If you are working with a designer, do them a favor and don't reduce image sizes, color-touch or crop the images unless you have a good deal of experience doing so.

Chapter 4
Should You Sell Online?

Deciding to sell online can be a big decision. In addition to choosing which products to sell, you also need to decide what sort of mechanism you will use to sell and how you will accept and process payment.

First, some terminology.

Cart: A cart system can indicate a few different things. It can be a full-fledged system embedded in your website that allows people to make purchases and that processes their credit cards. The cart system can also take the orders and then send them to a third party for payment and shipment processing. Because there are an array of options, from free to costly, you need to carefully define your cart needs before you commit to any one cart system.

SSL: A secure socket layer (SSL) certificate, also known as a security certificate, is a must if you are processing credit card orders on your website. SSL encrypts credit card and other data before it is sent over the internet. A website that supports SSL will have an address that starts with "https://". Never send sensitive data over a website that does not have an address of "https://."

Merchant Account: A merchant account processes the credit card orders that come through your cart and provides security and other services. Many merchant accounts can be quite pricey, as they charge a percentage fee for each order on top of standard credit card fees, plus a monthly fee to have the account. Some even charge extra fees if you *don't* sell a certain volume each month. Merchant accounts can be useful if you have a large number of products, high volume of sales, or very finite staff to take care of online sales. However, if you are a small company or have few products, a merchant account isn't usually necessary. The orders can be hand-processed on an in-store card unit or phone reader. Companies such as Square or PayPal essentially function as merchant accounts but are far cheaper to use.

How Are You Going to Sell Your Items?

There are essentially three options for selling online:
- Sell via a **third-party** site
- Sell via a few simple **payment buttons** (usually linking to PayPal)
- Sell via a full-fledged cart system

The more complex a system, the pricier it will be. If sales go well, you can always upgrade to a bigger cart system. For many small businesses, there is no need to have a large full-fledged cart straight-away; it simply isn't cost-effective.

Using a Third-party Company

There are thousands of third-party companies that you can use to sell your products and services. They run the gamut from print-on-demand clothing and books, to companies that maintain a stock of your products and handle distribution and fulfillment, to full-fledged stores where you can have your own mini-store.

Some of the more familiar ones include:

amazon.com

ebay.com

half.com

etsy.com

cafepress.com

zazzle.com

artfulhome.com

lulu.com

fineartamerica.com

These sites offer very few options in modifying looks or features, but they are designed for those with the least experience to use quickly and easily. The small fee they charge and fast set-up may be all you need to encourage you to dip your toe in the online commerce pool.

There are numerous sites targeting different groups to sell online. You may be able to sell your products or services through:

- A club or association site, like a Chamber of Commerce website.
- A professional website that requires membership and accreditation.
- A "Buy Local" page focusing on your city, county or state.
- Niche-market resellers.
- Wholesaler drop-ship sites which handle the resale of your products.

Many **third-party push-button website builder programs** also allow you to build your cart right along with the rest of the website. There is very little set-up required on your end, the package usually comes with some decent tech support, the cart system is usually cheaper to set up than a full-fledged cart on your website and often comes with some advertising. However, in the long run these carts can be more costly due to on-going fees. They cannot be tailored to your specific needs, nor will the tech support be able to provide you with help beyond their basic, set parameters. While these companies will also offer you exposure to a large audience, you will be competing with many other companies.

Third-party sites are ideal if:
- You only have a few products to sell.
- You don't want to be bothered with handling the transactions.

- Your product or service fits well on a third-party website. For instance, hand-made hats on etsy.com or books on amazon.com.
- You'd like to reach a large audience or start selling fast.
- You don't want to invest in a full cart system.
- Your products or services are only available for a set period of time or part of the year. For instance, you may only sell holiday decorations a few months of the year.

Third-party sites are also an excellent **addition** to many sites.

For instance:
- You may fulfill orders for paperback books via your website, but direct visitors to Amazon for the Kindle edition.
- Your website may carry prints and boxed notecards of your artwork, but original, one-of-a-kind pieces are sold through etsy.com.
- You may be considering sweatshirts with your club logo, but don't want to print a bunch and not have them sell, so you offer them through Cafe Press.
- You mostly do standard car repairs in your shop, but you have a small specialty store on Ebay selling vintage auto parts.
- You do most of your consulting one-on-one in your office, but you occasionally offer Skype services via vCita.com.

Before you sign up for any services, make sure you understand:
- What the fees will be to use their service.
- Whether you will also have to pay a portion of the sale in addition to a use fee.
- Whether your products or services are allowed.
- Whether you have to sign a contract for a set amount of time.
- The cancellation policies.
- How you will be paid, and how often.

Avoid sites that:

- Require a contract that has a set amount of time with no cancellation allowed, or a contract that requires additional fees to end the service.
- Has bad reviews online or at the Better Business Bureau.
- Has few other companies or products on the website.
- Claims exclusive rights to sell your product or service and doesn't allow sales or advertising elsewhere.
- Forces sellers to offer discounts or sales.
- Charges sellers for stocking or re-stocking.
- Charges additional fees to move money made from sales, such as charges to transfer money into a bank account.

Before you sign up with any third-party site, be sure to <u>read all the fine print</u>. It's small and hard to read for a reason.

Embedding Buttons or a Cart in Your Site, but Processing Elsewhere (Offsite Processing)

Another option is to have the buttons or cart for sales on your site, but to leave the actual processing to a third-party company. While there are merchant account systems that allow these sorts of sales, PayPal is by far the most popular option for this method.

PayPal allows you to set up an account and create buttons with quite a few choices, such as drop-down menus, various shipping options, sales tax settings for different states and more. The code it spits out can easily be pasted into a website.

This is ideal if:

- You only have a few products to sell.
- You want it quick and simple.

- You don't want to be bothered with handling some or all of the payment transaction.
- You don't want to invest in a full cart and security system.
- You don't need a lot of shipping or other options.
- You don't want to pay fees if you aren't making sales.
- You want to take credit card payments for products, donations, subscriptions, reoccurring fees, downloads or other services.
- You want to take as many forms of currency as possible, including direct cash transfer, all major credit cards and international currency.
- You want to know that the credit card numbers have already been approved, so you don't need to take additional steps to verify them.

There are a lot of terrific reasons to use PayPal: no fees unless you make a sale (and far lower than most other merchant accounts), shipping and tax are quick and easy to set up, as are purchase and cart buttons. PayPal takes virtually any credit card and can do bank transfers. Additionally, they take care of all the security, card approval and processing on their end.

PayPal does charge additional fees for advanced business services. It takes a few days for payments to get transferred out of your PayPal account into your bank. Their buttons are very basic and don't offer the functionality and flexibility for buying options a full-fledged cart system can offer. For instance, you can set up color or size on a button, but can't change the price based on size or quantity ordered.

However, PayPal can be used as the payment processing gateway for an advanced cart system on your website. Most large retailers offer PayPal as a way to make payments, in addition to standard credit card processing.

Setting up a Full-service Cart System

A full-service cart system can be very nice to have. Most carts are out-of-the-box products that install quickly and easily. They can be integrated into your design and have many options, with plug-ins that can be added. Also, many of these cart systems are free to use, like PrestaShop, OsCommerce, and Zen Cart. There are numerous free and very low-cost WordPress cart plug-ins that can be integrated in minutes.

These cart systems are highly customizable. They allow you the ability to offer combination products, custom product tailoring, discounts, coupons, an array of shipping and tax options, reporting, mailing labels, client accounts and much more. Generally, if you want it, it can be done.

While almost all the cart systems are free or very low cost, there is a cost in time and/or money to install, set up and maintain. In addition to installing a cart system, you need to add products, shipping rates, taxes, and images, and to test the system.

If you choose to have a merchant account, (e.g. at authorize.net), make sure your cart system is compatible with the merchant account before you sign anything. With many merchant accounts, or if you want to hand-process the credit card numbers, you will need an SSL certificate to encrypt the numbers, which can cost around $40-50 a year.

A full-service cart system is ideal if you:
- Have a large number of products for sale.
- Have staff devoted to online sales.
- You wish to have prices change on a product, depending on option selections, such as increase the price of a shirt by $5 if long-sleeved is chosen over short-sleeved.
- Have the budget to set up the cart system and pay fees associated with online sales.

- You wish to have advanced features, like orders that can be broken up into separate shipments.
- You want to allow a lot of options on products, such as the ability to choose different sleeve lengths and colors for a shirt.
- You want customers to have accounts where they can easily reorder products, get tracking IDs, check the status of an order and more.
- Allow varying types of products in one purchase, such as a digital download and a physical product.

—

Be realistic about how many products you are likely to sell starting out. I had a would-be client who fired me almost as soon as we began because I didn't have her "vision." I suggested we start by selling her books via PayPal, instead of installing an expensive cart system. She replied that she expected to sell at least 10,000 books a month. The publisher later told me that she actually sold around 10 books a month.

—

What Should I Sell Online?

Consider the following:
- How many products are you selling?
- Do you need lots of shipping options, such as overnight or overseas shipping?
- How many products do you expect to sell as you start up?
- Do your products offer any specialization options, such as engraving, author's signature, or tailoring?
- Do you plan to ship the products yourself, or have a third-party fulfillment service do it for you?

- Do the products need lots of options, such as sizes and colors?
- What sort of margin will you make on your sales after adding a cart?
- Do you already have a brick-and-mortar location that gives you an indication of what products are most popular?
- Do you want to allow people to pay fees, subscribe to a service or offer other intangibles?
- Do you want to sell downloads or other digital items?
- Are you prepared to do the bookkeeping for sales tax, quarterly taxes and other accounting-related activities? Will you use an accountant?
- Do you or your staff have the time to run online sales?
- Do you trust your staff to have access to your financial accounts?
- Will this be your only sales outlet, or will you be offering sales in other locations? For instance, are your products available in retail stores or at amazon.com?
- Will selling online affect your product or service pricing? Regardless of what means you use to sell online, you will still have to pay some sort of fee.

Bear in mind that if you have a large selection of products or services, you don't need to offer all of them for sale online at once. You may want to start with your best-sellers, then add more items if sales go well.

There are some products that lend themselves well to online sales, and others that are much more difficult.

Products that will sell well online can be quickly and easily restocked. They are easy to pack and ship and are non-perishable. Goods that are needed occasionally but hard to find in local stores, such as older replacement parts or exotic spices do well, as do commonly needed items that people would prefer not to shop around for. This includes books, shoes, clothing, housewares and other common items. Others items which have easily listed and detailed information, like a box of software, sell well online. Flat fees for a subscription or service, such as an hour massage or a year's magazine subscription also do well.

More difficult to sell online are products that often go out of stock or are one-of-a-kind objects, like art. Shipping can be a problem on objects that are large, fragile, ungainly or heavy. Conversely, some items may cost more in shipping than the item itself, such as stickers or tubes of lipstick. Perishable goods, items that you cannot ship to certain states or countries and goods that must be experienced in person, such as fabrics, eyewear, or fragrances also may not do as well. Items or services that don't have a finite set price can be very tricky. For instance, a service that needs to have an estimate quoted, depending on the complexity of the job.

If your primary product or service doesn't lend itself well to online sales, you can still offer ancillary items. For instance, you are unlikely to sell a lot of furnaces online. However, you may do well with an online shop selling replacement parts, filters and digital copies of repair manuals.

Some items really need to be experienced in person prior to purchase. You can encourage sales of these sorts of items by offering samples, either for sale or upon request.

These may include:
- A sampler pack of soap chips or miniature perfume vials.
- A sampler pack of chocolates, coffees or other confections.
- Samples of paint, tile, wood, fabric or wallpaper.
- Embedded sound or video clips of your music.
- Video samples showing your product from different angles, in use and in different types of lighting.

Some companies find that their sampler offerings are their most popular items because shoppers like variety.

If you do offer free items of some sort, require users to provide some basic contact information so you can add them to an email list. Then you can send them the occasional email nudge about the products they have sampled.

How Do I Describe My Products?

Once you've decided what you are going to be selling online, you need to come up with product descriptions. Like any page content, this text should be descriptive. Remember that the viewer can't pick up the item and experience it firsthand. Your item descriptions need to create a strong idea in the viewer's mind.

The more clearly you describe your products and attributes, the more appealing they will be and the less likely they will be returned.

Be sure to include:
- A description of what each item is used for along with reasons why someone should purchase it.
- Each item's dimensions (height, weight, depth), including dimensions for different configurations (as with a foldout sofa).
- Each item's weight, which is particularly pertinent if you need to charge additional fees for shipping.
- The colors options available. If your colors are not clear standards (black, white, red), have both color swatches and some descriptions of the colors. For instance, you may say "lilac - a soft, dusty light purple" to help clarify.
- A sizing chart for any clothes, shoes, hats, jewelry or other items worn on the body. As there is no standard sizing for small, medium, large, etc., use inches or centimeters to give all

pertinent measurements. This includes hat circumference, lengths of sleeves and inseam, lengths of necklaces, bracelets and dangling earrings, calf size for boots, conversions for European sizes and any other "generic" sizing that would confuse a potential buyer. An XL hoodie from China and one from Wisconsin can be *yards* apart in size.

- Information that a buyer would be able to read off a package, were they holding it in their hands. This includes book synopses, bullet points about features, ingredients, required tools to assemble an item and any other packaging text.
- Information on whether an item comes pre-assembled. If not, include estimated assembly time and tools needed.
- Terms or conditions specific to the product.
- Descriptions of any scents or tastes as accurately as you can. For instance, "a dark, slightly bitter chocolate with nutty undertones" is far more descriptive than "dark chocolate."
- If the item for sale is not a tangible product that will be shipped, include information on how the purchaser will receive it. For instance, tell them a link to the digital product will be available in their email receipt once the order is processed.
- Include time limits on payment for a service or product. For instance, gift certificates are good for one year from purchase date.

Pricing

Determining how and what you are going to sell online can depend on a number of costs: your product costs, overhead, profit margins, shipping and handling fees, taxes, bulk rates and more. Factoring in these costs will help you determine how many products to sell online, how much to charge, how much of a discount you can offer and how much you need to charge for shipping and handling.

What you should consider:

- What is base cost of your product or service?
- Can you save money by encouraging credit card payment? For instance, is it cheaper to take online payments than to send out physical invoices?
- Can you sell digital versions of your product, saving you production cost? For instance, can you sell an ebook, mp3 version of an album or access to a training video?
- Can you have clients pre-pay for services, such as buying a punch card for drop-in classes?
- Will you sell more if you offer bulk discounts? Do you want to offer unit price reductions on larger orders? If so, will the discount you offer be large enough to be appealing and not hurt your bottom line?
- Will the cost to provide or sell the product go up or down if you start selling online? For instance, you may be able to buy material at wholesale rates with enough online sales, so prices can decrease. Or you may need to hire additional staff to process orders, which will make prices increase.
- How much will packaging cost? This includes boxes or envelopes, padding material, print material you may include (such as a catalog or postcards), printing invoices and labels.
- How much will handling cost? How long will it take to print labels and invoices, pack the items and either meter the items for postage or drive them to a mailing location?
- Will you offer gift wrapping?
- Are you interested in having the option of C.O.D., school or government purchase orders or check payments?
- What cards do you want to accept? Are you only interested in VISA, Mastercard and perhaps American Express? Do you want any sort of debit, prepaid or other credit card to be accepted?
- You will need to factor into the product price all of your costs: the

cart, hosting, domain, design, security, credit card processing fees and other web-related costs.

Don't forget, anything related to building the cart and website is tax deductible!

Shipping

Shipping really seems to trip people up. Figuring out what to charge can get tricky. But knowing what options you need *up front* can make setting up and choosing your online sales options much easier. It can also keep you from losing money on your shipping from unexpected costs.

What are your shipping rates? When in doubt, use the calculators on the USPS, UPS and other shipping pages: plug in weights, ship times and locations to get ballpark estimates.

- Will you ship only to the continental United States, all of the United States, military addresses, Canada/Mexico, or anywhere in the world?
- Do any of your products need to be expedited (e.g. because they are perishable?)
- Can any of your products not be shipped at certain times of the year (e.g. milk chocolate in summer, tropical plants in winter)?
- Is it legal to ship your products (e.g., firearms, alcohol, agricultural produce) to all states/countries?
- Can you send any of your products at the media rate?
- Will a signature be required on delivery?
- Do you need tracking and/or delivery confirmation?
- Do you want to offer your customers multiple carrier options, such as USPS, UPS and DHL?
- Do you wish to offer in-store pick-up?

- Do you want to offer free shipping when the purchase exceeds a certain dollar amount?
- Will your shipping be based on the total weight of the items, the number of items or a percentage of the total, or will you charge a flat rate per order?
- Will some items require additional shipping charges due to size, shape, or weight?

Terms and Conditions

It is unlikely that most visitors to your website will read the terms and conditions. However, they are often vital to you after someone has made a purchase. While you may want to include terms and conditions on specific items, you should also have blanket terms and conditions for all purchases made through your website.

These may include:
- How long a purchaser has to return an item. For instance, an item may be returned for a refund within 7 days of receipt or exchanged within 30 days.
- The condition in which the item must be returned. For instance, new shoes with original packaging can be returned for a refund. Shoes with signs of wear can be exchanged for store credit.
- Who will pay for return shipping—you or the purchaser. Will you waive shipping fees on an exchanged or damaged item?
- Whether or not the item can be exchanged for a comparable one.
- What if the exchanged item costs more or less than the original item?
- Whether or not a purchase be refunded.
- What items cannot be returned or exchanged. For instance, items with custom engraving cannot be returned or exchanged.

Chapter 5
Should You Blog?

Blogs started out as online diaries. People would post stories and thoughts and readers could comment on them. Blogging is a terrific way to share information with customers, clients, website members and others. It can give a personal feel to the site, help you connect directly with your clients and offer all sorts of informative additions that don't fit into the standard website framework.

A blog enables you to:
- Share in-depth information about your products or services.
- Relate your experience running your business or providing a service.
- Offer your expertise.
- Initiate a conversation and obtain feedback.
- Test the market for a new product or service.
- Offer advice or tips on your products, such as assembling or repairing them.
- Create a product, such as a collection of online articles available only to members.
- Post a serialized story or set of articles.
- Entice visitors to return to your website regularly, even though most of the website is static.

Just because you now *have* a blog doesn't mean you now have additional time in your day to *write* the blog.

A blog is a terrific way to interact directly with your visitors, but it can be also be a time-suck. If you plan to blog regularly, keep these rules in mind:

45

- If you are spending time blogging, something else has to give. Ideally, you will block out some time for blogging. For instance, every other Friday morning, 9:00-9:30.
- Make sure your topics are pertinent to your business and advance your business goals. What actions will blogging encourage your readers to take?
- Don't name names or get into too much detail. For instance, if you are posting a funny anecdote, don't use the names of persons involved or give specific details about the incident. You may find it hilarious, but your subjects may not.
- Don't bash the competition or products you sell. Keep it positive.
- Maintain a list of blog post ideas for when you can't think of one.
- If you are using a CMS system such as WordPress, you can write a batch of blog posts in advance, then set them up to post at regular intervals.
- Don't post anything you wouldn't say to someone's face.
- If you don't plan to post often, don't show dates on the posts. You can call the area "articles" or something else, and simply post occasionally.
- Keep the posts related to your business. Posts about personal matters, hot-button topics like religion and politics, and fluffy filler like YouTube videos of cats have no place on a professional business blog.
- If people aren't reading your blog, you hate doing it and/or it isn't serving any purpose in furthering your business goals, **stop blogging**.

—

The most unprofessional blog I ever saw was that of a PR/Marketing professional who was working with a client of mine. I was curious to see who her other clients were, so I popped over to her business website. Instead of a standard "Welcome" page, she had a string of venomous posts about her divorce and her ex. Classy.

—

Blog Commenting

Should you allow people to comment on your blog? A blog allows you to have a conversation with readers about the topics on which you are writing. They may give you invaluable feedback and lots of great ideas, kudos and suggestions. However, the world is full of trolls and spammers who are looking for opportunities to gain access to your website. They want to spam you or use your website to spread their message. Or, they are just jerks looking to spew hate. (BTW, if you discover the cure for stupid, please email me!)

At the very least, require commenters to fill out a form to prove they are human, via CAPTCHA or other confirmation methods. Do not auto-post comments. You should approve each one before it goes live. Moderating comments take both time and effort, so consider the pros and cons carefully.

Before allowing comments, consider:
- Do you have the time to read and approve comments promptly?
- Do you wish engage in conversation?
- Why do you want people to comment? Is it to obtain feedback on your products, to find out what new products or services customers would like to see, to collect testimonials or to take questions or complaints?
- What will you do if comments are negative or inappropriate?

Chapter 6
How Should Your Page Look?

Once you have an idea of what sort of content your website should contain, how many links and other features such as a blog or cart system, and so forth, you need to decide how it will look.

The design of the website should come **after** your have worked out your content. Why? The design of a website is there to make the website easier to understand and navigate, to illustrate what the website is about and make it visually more attractive and cohesive.

If you start with a design, then try to shoehorn in your content, you will end up with a big mess. You may have far too many or too few links to fit into a specific design. The colors or fonts you choose may make no sense in the context of what the website is about. There may be no room for social media icons, a search bar or an embedded cart.

How the website should look is an area that pulls a lot of people up short. They know what their website should say and what they want visitors to do, but how do they make their website design reflect this?

The design of a website should aid the visitor in finding information and give visual clues to what the website is about. It should not make it more confusing or distract from the content.

What Does "Design" Mean?

The design of a website includes:
- The color palette.
- The placement of areas of the website: for instance, logo at the top

left corner, featured products in a sidebar, address in a footer.
- Textures and backgrounds.
- Placement of illustrative images, such as product shots or images that simply make the page more attractive.
- Details like artwork on buttons, frames around images, rounded corners and other little touches.
- Font styles, colors, and decoration.
- Style of navigation including links and menus.
- Visual features like photo galleries, portfolios, slideshows or embedded videos.

Elements to consider for your site:

What actions do you want visitors to take? Your prime focus should be on what you want the visitors to do. This may be buying a product, getting directions, reading about your services, or buying a subscription. This top action should be front and center on the homepage and always available as an option on all subsequent pages.

Build around your logo. Your design should use a similar color palette and the same fonts so they tie together. Nothing looks more haphazard than a logo and website design that are completely different in appearance.

Use colors that reflect the tone of your business. Gentle pastels, vibrant jewel tones, professional muted tones? Not sure? Check out colourlovers.com/palettes for ideas.

Textures, borders and background wallpaper can add extra depth and detail to the website.

Do you want any animation or movement on the website, such as Flash, embedded videos, links or a logo that slides in? Remember, the more movement on a page, the longer it takes to load. Also, many people find movement on a page distracting in a bad way.

What font lettering reflects your business? Elegant script, blocky poster text, professional serif type? Not sure? Check out dafont.com for ideas.

How many links do you want visible on the website? If you have only a few pages, you will want all the links in a menu bar. However, if you have dozens or hundreds of pages, the top links should always be visible, with lesser pages available from drop-down menus. For instance, your top link may be About Us, with Press, Our History and Our Employees dropping down below.

What is your competition doing? Are there design standards that are expected for your industry? Do you like them and do they seem to work? Can you make your website better and more attractive than these standards? Let's say all your competitors use soft pastels and dreamy pictures. Would using strong colors and bold, eye-catching images set you apart and make your company seem stronger? Or would it be too jarring to the target audience?

If you aren't the one designing the site, conveying what you'd like to a designer or employee can be tricky. What you like may seem nebulous. Finding websites with elements you like is a terrific way to help articulate what you want. You may tell them "I like how clean and simple this website is," or "I love the colors on this site," or "I'd like two lines of links along the top, like this page." You may also say, "Don't use any colors or blinking art like this!"

When researching what you'd like for a website design, don't hold yourself to looking at sites in your own industry. You may be a florist, but love the website of your hairstylist or an art gallery.

When I design a website or logo, I always reject the first idea that comes to me since that is invariably the generic standard. You want to stand out, not be a clone.

Look at the sites of your competition with a critical eye. Are they attractive or dull? Are they easy to navigate or do you get lost? Are they professional, or do they look clunky or outdated? Make notes on what you'd do to make it better if it were your website. Then one-up 'em!

Google terms like "inspiring web design" to find samples of great pages. Websites like siteinspire.com, awwwards.com, webdesign-inspiration.com, pinterest.com and more can give you a wide range of well-designed sites. They can also help you narrow down the terms and styles you like. Do you want a minimalist site, or one rich with detail? Would you like an art deco feel, or perhaps post-modernist?

Flash Animation

I'll admit, I'm not a fan. Flash had potential when it was first introduced, but the number of places where Flash animation is used intelligently is nearly negligible. I've seen a few beautiful and clever animations. One allowed you to explore an Egyptian tomb and another the decks of a pirate ship. Unfortunately, the vast majority of Flash consists of a company's logo and some products bouncing around the screen to canned music or cartoon sounds. This is neither compelling, interesting nor useful.

Flash has its own programming language and can be tricky to work with. Creating even 10-15 seconds of animation can be very labor-intensive and expensive. It is most definitely not a program you simply pick up and run with. More often than not, visitors skip the flash animation. Search engines have a hard time crawling (reading) the content of Flash. And, since 2010 Mac has refused to support Flash (apple.com/hotnews/thoughts-on-flash/). That's a pretty darn big target market.

If you do want Flash animation in your site, make sure that Flash is the best option for presenting your information.

Reasons to include Flash may include:
- Allowing viewers to take a self-guided virtual tour or "move around" in an area.
- Showing dynamically how something looks, moves, changes or adapts.
- Showing something that is already animated, such as having a cartoon character move.

Generally, there are better ways to present your information than in Flash, and most of those alternatives cost less, too.

Where and Why Should I Add Video Content?

For a while, the new hotness was having a video of your company president walking around the home page, blabbing about how welcome the visitor was and how awesome the company was. To be honest, I'm not *totally* sure what they were saying. I was usually clicking frantically for a way to make it stop, pounding the mute button and yelling, "shut up, Shut Up, SHUT UP!" This phase, thankfully, seems to have passed.

If you include video in your site, it should have a specific purpose. It shouldn't be there merely so you can say you have a video. A video requires a great deal more interaction on the visitor's part; they need to watch and listen, hit play or pause, adjust volume or skip around. A video also takes far longer to load and watch than simple text or images. So make it worthwhile for your visitor to watch video content.

Videos on a website can:

- Demonstrate how to do something that is too complex to explain through writing or that has multiple steps.
- Illustrate features or details not easily shown in a static image.
- Give a tour of a location.
- Demonstrate proof of a product's worth, usefulness or durability (hello <u>willitblend.com</u>!).
- Make dull reading more interesting with audio or visual cues.
- Show examples of an item from different angles or in different lighting, such as a piece of artwork.
- Show samples of your ability to speak publicly, dance, perform music, etc.
- Embed news stories, interviews or shows that feature your business.

As with all photography, make sure that there is plenty of good lighting, a plain background and good audio quality. No one wants to watch a dark video that bounces around, with murky sound and the occasional weird crinkle. Do it well, or don't do it at all.

—

I had a client who wanted to start a vlog (video blog). I told her to film somewhere without any distracting background or ambient sounds (like traffic). While she followed the spirit of the advice, the videos she sent looked and sounded like they were filmed in a coat closet...
because they had been.

—

Also, be sure that the employees, clients or customers you are using in your video have agreed to be filmed. Some may not want to appear simply because they are having a bad hair day. Others may have religious or cultural objections, or may even be trying to keep a low-profile from an ex who is stalking them. Be respectful and don't push if they say "no."

Using YouTube

Unless you have a very specific reason not to, put your videos up on youtube.com, then embed them in your website.

Why use YouTube?

- YouTube does an excellent job converting videos uploaded to the website into a format that can load quickly and play on virtually any browser or platform.
- YouTube comes with some rudimentary editing software.
- Videos are large and offloading them to another server with a lot of support is a good way to save on hosting fees, especially if you plan to have a lot of videos.
- YouTube is known worldwide. The viewer will likely find your video through YouTube, then come back to your website for more information.
- You can create a channel and have a whole series of videos, so if visitors like one they can easily watch more.
- Visitors can rate your videos and make comments. Of course, you want/hope for positive ratings and comments!
- A really good video can go viral and be shared all over the net and on social media. It is much easier (and easier on your website's bandwidth) if videos are watched on YouTube. Of course, you will want to direct people from the video back to your website.

While there has been some talk about YouTube as a **money-making revenue stream**, the reality is that a very, very few make any real money from or by advertising on YouTube. Most make almost nothing. Literally, as in a fraction of a cent. So unless you are creating professionally filmed and produced videos and they have the sort of content that tends to go viral, it's unlikely they will garner the sort of following that brings in income. Your video on how to install a toilet may be very much appreciated by the hundred people who watched it, but the chances of it getting the same amount of attention as the video with the cat in a shark costume riding a Roomba while being chased by a duck, is pretty darn slim.

Chapter 7
How Should You Choose a Domain Name and Host?

Now that you know what should be on your website and how you will be creating or acquiring that content, you need to decide where this website will reside. I know, I know, "On the interwebs." But what will the domain name of the website be and where will the website data be hosted? (And what the heck are they?)

How Do I Choose a Domain Name?

Your domain name is your website address, also known as your *uniform resource locator* (URL). It is the way you direct people to your website - kind of like a street address on the information superhighway.

Choosing a domain name may not seem too complicated, but there are a few things that can trip you up:

When choosing a domain name, consider:
- **Is your domain name available?** To check, go to any domain registry, such as godaddy.com or who.is to see if the domain you want is available to buy. Just because there isn't a website currently at a domain doesn't mean it is available. It may be owned by someone who hasn't gotten around to using it yet. However, a registry will tell you if it is available for purchase.
- **Expect to pay in the vicinity of $10 per year for a domain.** Anything more than $15 for a standard domain is a rip-off.
- **If your first choice isn't available, what are some permutations that may be acceptable?** For instance, you can add a hyphen (acme-co.com), add a location (acme-wisconsin.com), or use a different extension, such as .net instead of .com (acme.net).

Use .org if you are a non-profit organization. I am not a fan of other extensions, such as .biz or .us (the United States country code). They aren't as memorable as .com or .net, and shady companies often use them.

- **Is your domain name memorable?** If it is too long (acmepaintingcompany-madisonwisconsin.com) people will have a hard time remembering it. The same is true with more obscure abbreviations or acronyms (apcmadwi-omg.com). Keep the name succinct and memorable.

- **Use *your* name instead of your business's name.** If customers know you or your product by name, rather than the company, have a domain such as johnsmith.com. (For example, the Cheerios cereal brand is more widely known than General Mills, the company that makes Cheerios.) The domain with your name can also forward (bounce visitors) to the domain with your business name.

- **You can have as many domains as you wish.** You can have different versions of your website or simply forward visitors from satellite sites to the main website.

- **If you are looking to reach a wide audience, a more generic name will attract people from all over.** In these circumstances, paying a premium fee for a domain name *may* be a good idea. While domain names are initially available for a very low fee, there are companies that make their money snagging highly desirable names and reselling them for a much higher price – hundreds or even thousands of dollars. However, if you want to be the world's leading supplier of widgets, you may need to pay the hefty fee to get the domain widgets.com.

- **Just because it is your *business name,* doesn't mean it is your *domain name!*** You may be the owner of Acme Painting Company, but that doesn't mean you have automatic rights to that name. If someone else bought the name legitimately (like

Acme Painting Company, Peoria), they can use it, within the limits of the law. Illegal use includes others pretending to be you, posting false or slanderous information, or selling fake products.

- **If you have someone else, such as a designer, register your domain for you, ask that your company name be put on the contact information.** This way you can access the domain at a later date, just in case you are no longer working with that designer.

- **The same applies if you are having an employee register the domain.** Make sure the contact information is the company's generic phone, email and address and that they use the company credit card. If the employee leaves (especially if they leave in a huff) and have their name and contact information on the domain, they can be considered the owner. Trying to get a domain back in this sort of situation can be expensive, time-consuming and often futile.

- **Write down or print the login and password information for your domain.** Put it in a drawer. No, really. At some point in the future, you will be glad you did.

- Make sure your domain is **spelled correctly** when registering!

- **Make sure your domain name doesn't spell something embarrassing!** These are real domains:
  www.whorepresents.com — Who represents: Finding agents who represent famous people.
  www.expertsexchange.com — Experts exchange: A website where experts exchange information.
  www.therapistfinder.com — Therapist finder: A website where you can find therapists.
  www.penisland.net — Pen island: A shop selling pens.
  ~ From Episode 9 of the "E" TV series QI.

I was working on a get-out-the-vote campaign. The password and login they had given me didn't work. I double-checked the ownership of the domain they were about to send to a half million households. You guessed it, they didn't own it and it wasn't available.

Most importantly:

Make sure your contact information is kept up-to-date on your domain. If the email is no longer current, you will not get renewal notices. If the domain is not renewed in a set period of time, it will expire. Someone else can then buy name and put up a website at the address at the address. There is virtually nothing you can do in a case like this. You lost it and someone else bought it.

If the email is no longer valid and you don't have the login information, but the phone number, address, credit card or other information is still valid, you can sometimes get access to your domain through a phone call to the registry company. Other times a registered letter is required. This is time-consuming and irritating—avoid it if at all possible.

How Do I Choose a Host?

A host is a company that owns computers called servers. Servers hold web data and "serve" it up to visitors. Servers also transfer emails. When you sign up for hosting, you are essentially renting a small bit of space on a server to hold your website and pass on emails to and from you. Hosts are like apartments—if you don't like one, you can pack up your data and move. Also like an apartment, if you leave and turn in your keys, then come back a week later asking for the stuff you forgot here, you will find that your couch (or in this case, old emails) are long gone. Make sure you have back-ups and transfer *all* files before canceling a host.

Hosting is one of those services whose quality is hard to judge. On the whole, you will generally have the best luck with either small local providers or large companies whose main business is hosting, such as Godaddy or Network Solutions. A quick online search for "hosting reviews" can give you a good idea of what experiences other people have had. Phone companies are notorious for the abysmal quality of their hosting, as are companies who add hosting services as an afterthought.

What constitutes "good" and "bad" hosting? If you have a good host, you will simply forget about them. Your website will be up and load fast, emails will send and receive, and you won't be inundated with spam. On the rare occasion you need assistance, you can reach tech support fast, they are knowledgeable, polite, speak good English and fix the problem within 24 hours. While there is plenty to dislike about Godaddy as a company, their phone support is unbeatable.

With a bad host, your website will be down for periods of time. Emails will be blocked or be bounced back. Databases will become corrupted, software will not be maintained and not be up to date, and sites will not be properly backed up so they can be restored. Tech support will be hard to reach and useless if you do get a human. In the worst case scenario, the host will also deny any of the above problems are happening. If you are unhappy with your host, pack up your website and move elsewhere.

Hosting will cost in the range of $6-15 a month and should include a few email accounts. Be leery of anything cheaper or free; there is almost always a catch. Perhaps they are simply a lousy host, or the website you've made is on their proprietary software, so you can't take it somewhere else. Other times, there will be banner ads plastered all over your website. It only costs a few dollars a month to look professional.

Email Accounts

Almost all hosting packages now come with at least one email account.

Avoid any that charge extra for an email; it's a rip-off. Even if you are the sole owner of your business, you can have more than one email account. You may want a contact@mydomain.com email that receives messages from the contact form, another workshops@mydomain.com account used just on workshop sign-ups and another general info@mydomain.com account.

Having an email at your domain name is a good idea for a couple of reasons:

- It looks more professional to have a matching email and domain – me@mydomain.com.
- The matching email reinforces your domain name in the viewer's memory.
- You have control over the account and don't need to rely on a third-party.

Of course, if you prefer, you can have your domain email forward to something like a gmail account. Gmail can even be set up to be your main email program, but still show your domain email address on the email's To and From headers.

Chapter 8
How Will The Website Get Built?

So, now that you have a good idea of who the website is for and what should be on it, you need to decide **how** this website will be built.

There are three options:
- build it yourself with an online **point-and-click** program
- build it yourself by learning a more **complex program or software**
- **hire someone** else to do it

Some things to consider:
- What is the budget?
- How much time do you or your employees have to build a website?
- How soon does it need to be completed?
- Do you or your employees have any experience building a website?
- Do you or your employees have any interest in building a website?
- Do you or your employees have an aptitude for learning new computer programs or languages?

Using an Online Point-and-Click Program

The first option, **using a point-and-click program,** is very tempting when starting out. Many large hosting companies offer programs that promise you can build a website in mere hours. Other paid services have their entire business model built around point-and-click sites. They offer a combination of hosting and an editing program, plus support, for a fee.

These are a good option when you have very little time, money, skill, interest... or a combination thereof.

Some sites that are ideal for a point-and-click program:

- Event sites that will not need to be up long – *graduations, weddings, reunions.*
- Sites where a number of members are expected to be able to post with little to no training.
- One-time sales sites, such as a house, auction or community garage sale.
- Sites that need to be completed as fast as possible, with all other considerations being secondary.

The point-and-click programs have many positive aspects. They are often free or very cheap to use. They are fast and easy to learn. Often you can put together an entire website in a matter of hours. Most come with a few attractive templates. The paid ones often have excellent tech support, especially if they are available through a large hosting company.

Conversely, these programs can also have some drawbacks. The free point-and-click programs often require you to display prominent advertising. Features outside the standard package are often not possible, or cost more to add. While there is usually some leeway in changing color, fonts and background colors, the rest of the website design is usually held rigidly to the prefab template layout. Your website will therefore appear very similar to other sites.

In addition, many point-and-click programs use proprietary software. If you want to leave and take your website elsewhere, the framework or code for your website can't be moved to a new host. All you can take is your text and images, then rebuild your website elsewhere.

Learn a Web Design Software Program or Content Management System (CMS)

The second option, **learning a more complex program**, also has its appeal. Many people enjoy the learning process and the satisfaction of creating their own website from scratch. They feel they have control over their website and like the immediacy of being able to make their own changes.

Learning to write HTML and CSS, plus languages like PHP or Javascript, may seem passé with the prevalence of push-button programs; 99% of the time everything will work just fine. However, being able to go in and fix a bug or strange formatting problem by hand is invaluable that one time it all goes wonky. Taking the time to learn at least the basic formatting of the code can save you hours of misery later on.

Many hosts offer automatic installation of a **Content Management Systems (CMS)** with a hosting package. CMSes can be wonderful things. They offer a great deal more flexibility in both appearance and functionality for a website. Additionally, most are open-source and free to install and edit. However, if you don't have any experience setting up a CMS and a database, you may need the host to do this for you.

By far the easiest and most popular CMS to use is **WordPress**. WordPress started out as a free blogging platform. You could sign up for an account and start publishing posts within minutes because it was so easy and intuitive to use. The WordPress platform was so well loved that people demanded more and more features. Eventually, a stand-alone version was spun off so anyone could download it and install it on their server. This way, you could use WordPress on your domain (mydomain.com) as opposed to having to have an address at WordPress (mydomain.wordpress.com). There are thousands of free and paid plug-ins and templates available to use on WordPress. This is both a blessing and a curse, since sorting through them can be very time-consuming.

Other CMSes include Drupal and Joomla. Both offer many of the same features as WordPress and some specialized ones. All are free to use and have many ways for them to be expanded. At some point in your research you mind find that one or another of these CMSes is the ideal way for you to go for your specific website. In general, most beginners will find WordPress and its backend administration area the easiest to work with and use for their first website.

A CMS is often the ideal solution if you want to create and work on your own site, and want to have a great deal of control over functionality and appearance. You can start basic and expand and edit your website as you gain experience.

With a CMS, you have total control over the website. As long as you are using a non-proprietary CMS, you can move the website to any host you'd like. The top CMSes allow you to access and edit any of the code in any way you'd like. There are thousands of free and very affordable plugins that allow you to extend the functionality your website in any way imaginable–shopping carts, contact forms, image or video galleries, blogs and more. There are almost as many free, editable templates to change your website's appearance. These also can be edited and changed in any way you'd like to make your website totally unique.

While the CMS offers you almost total freedom to make your website look and function exactly as you wish, learning the skills needed for these changes are far more difficult and time-consuming. CMSes require a database to be set up and managed, a skill far beyond most beginners. To edit a website's appearance requires knowledge of cascading style sheets (CSS). Editing the website code and functionality requires knowledge of programming languages like PHP or ASP.

Many large hosts offer installation of a CMS and database so these more complex set-up steps aren't necessary. They may also offer some technical support. However, beyond some documentation for basic fixes of common problems, direct support may be costly.

If you are comfortable learning some new skills and building on them as you advance, a CMS is a great way to go.

Want to learn more on your own? Check out lynda.com for training videos on every level. Stackoverflow.com and wordpress.stackexchange.com are also wonderful resources for coding help of all sorts.

Hire a Web Designer or Web Development Company

If you want a professional website with a unique design, lots of features, personalized support and fast turnaround, a professional designer or design company is the way to go.

The options are fast, good or cheap. Pick any two.

When you hire an outside company, you have professionals working for you. They will help you clarify the scope of your project and what your needs are. A professional design company will answer your questions. They will build a website to specifications and make any modifications you want. Additionally, a professional can give you advice on areas of the website that may never have occurred to you. You will devote much less time to the website with the majority of the work being done for you.

Of course, a professional design company will need to know the full scope of the project and what it will entail before they can start.

Conveying what may seem like nebulous ideas can be very difficult. If this is all new to you, it can often be hard to tell if the professionals what you need. This is why you need to lay out and plan as much about your website as you can *before* you first meet with a design company.

How Do you Hire a Web Designer?

Hiring a web designer or web development company can be as nerve-wracking as trying to learn how to create the website yourself. How will you know if they are any good? Will they complete the website as requested? How much will it cost? What if it goes over budget? Who owns the website?

A good designer can make any website attractive and professional, regardless of the industry.

—

I had a client who wanted me to come to her company meeting on a Saturday. I told her I couldn't, as I was getting married. She suggested Sunday. I told her I was leaving on my honeymoon. She huffily told me, "Well, you can easily reschedule that by a few days."

I fired her on the spot.

—

Some things that characterize a good, honest company (usually):
- They will ask a lot of questions!
- They won't charge for initial consultation.
- They won't quote a number for the website until they have gotten your requirements.

- They will provide a written agreement with cost and time estimate and include a list of the services they will provide.
- They can show you samples of their work, even if they are only student projects.
- They can provide contacts and references from happy clients.

Dos and Don'ts for Discussing Your Website with a Designer:
- Do give as much information as you can provide about the site, content, target market, and features needed and desired. Don't expect the designer to guess or just "know."
- Do be honest about your budget and timeline. Often a website can be completed in phases as money becomes available. *Hint: "tomorrow" and "$10" are really not options.*
- Be sure to discuss cost and time overrun–*before* they overrun.
- Do consider how much help you need. If you are just starting out and are very small, a solo freelancer can do the job affordably and fast. If you are a larger company, need a large and complex cart system or are revamping a big system, a web development firm with a team of employees may be needed. Of course, rates increase with the size of the firm you are hiring.
- Don't immediately start using abbreviations, acronyms or slang from your business with the designer. Just because she is now working for you doesn't mean she has full understanding of your business.
- Don't automatically assume that the designer understands other things about your company, such as who the staff members are, what they do and their personality quirks.
- Do read any contracts or proposals provided before you sign anything. Claiming you "didn't know" or "didn't read" them in court holds as much water as a paper bag.
- Do make sure all your questions and concerns have been clarified before you sign anything.

- Don't hire anyone whose portfolio is unattractive to you. If you find nothing appealing in any of their designs, it is unlikely they will create something for you that you will like.
- You don't need to hire locally. There are designers all over the world that can make you a great, affordable website. (I've yet to meet 80% of my clients face-to-face.)
- Don't be afraid to contact the webmasters of sites you really like. While you don't want to be derivative, finding a designer whose style resonates with you is a great way to start. If the experience was a good one, the other company will be more than happy to share the designer's name and business information. If the experience wasn't good, they may give you a quiet warning you wouldn't have gotten anywhere else.
- Don't feel bad about Googling your potential design company. They may seem lovely at the initial consultation, but if there are numerous complaints at the Better Business Bureau or elsewhere, be wary. People rarely go out of their way to file a complaint or take a matter to small claims court; this is a good flag that the company may not be the best and there were significant problems.
- Do expect that you will need to provide a down-payment at the signing of the contract and before the designer will begin work.
- Don't be afraid to offer a trade of service or goods. However, be realistic about what you are offering. A designer may jump at a trade for house-painting or doggy daycare. They will probably be much less enthusiastic about being paid in decorative silk scarves (I sure wasn't).
- If you get a few proposals from different companies, it is perfectly fine to tell the other designers that you aren't using them. It happens all the time and we'd prefer a nice notice rather than to to be left hanging.
- Be sure to discuss deadlines. Design companies will be working

with lots of clients at once, so while they may quote 40 hours for your site, it is unlikely to be done in one week.

And very importantly:

Don't ask for "spec" work. Spec work is essentially asking a designer to do free work with the idea that you may, or may not, hire them for more work if you like it. From a designer's perspective, this is akin to going into a restaurant and demanding a free appetizer, then stating that you will order and pay for a dinner later if you like it. Maybe. Or maybe you'll just take the freebie and leave. Asking for spec work from a true professional will make them very leery of working for you. In all likelihood, the only designers who will take spec work are those that you really don't want to hire.

Note: If you are in a creative business yourself, you may have a very clear idea of what you would like. Perhaps you even have a design put together in Illustrator or Photoshop, but simply don't know how to convert it to a web page. Tell your design company up front about your desire to use your own design. They should be happy to adapt your work to the web. You may feel it is unprofessional to tell another creative person how to design something. But it is far more frustrating for them to try time and time again to create the vision in your head. In all likelihood, you'll end up bringing out this idea days or weeks into the process, further irritating the designer. It's **your** site, have it made the way **you** want it!

—

I spent an hour and half on the phone with a would-be client discussing her project. At the end of the conversation, she asked me, "So, could you recommend someone else who would do all of this, but cheaper?"

—

70

Chapter 9

How Will You Update the Website?

Keeping your website up to date is very important. Search engine bots regularly sweep through your website. They look at all the content on your website they can access and categorize it for searches. They also compare it with past versions of your website. If your website hasn't been updated in months or years, you are not only less likely to get repeat visitors, but over time, fewer new visitors will be sent your way. Your website will appear to be dead—no signs of life to show that anyone is still maintaining it.

You certainly don't have to add new products every week, or blog or post articles all the time. However, some general maintenance done at least a few times a year is necessary. Not only does it ensure that your website looks alive and kicking to the search engines, but it will also show visitors that are you are engaged, professional and very much still in business.

Regular upkeep may include:
- Removing past dates/events and adding new ones.
- Updating copyright.
- Removing unavailable products, or adding new ones.
- Adding new staff or removing old.
- Updating contact information.
- Updating shipping rates.
- Updating or adding to company history/information.
- Updating forms, white papers, spec or material data handling sheets.
- Reading through content to make sure it is still pertinent.
- Adding articles, newsletters, press or awards.
- Adding or removing logos and links of member groups.
- Checking outside links to member groups, recommended links,

71

sister/partner companies and retailers.
- Updating job openings.
- Making sure all retailer and wholesaler information is up-to-date.

Depending on how your website has been created, you or your staff may do the updates. If you have your website built by a third-party company, like a web developer, be sure to let them know that you wish to make updates in the future. Ask for login/password access and clear instructions or training on how to do the updates.

If one employee is in charge of updates, make sure you have copies of any instructions and passwords, *before* she leaves the company.

If you plan to have a third-party company make the changes, be sure to present the changes in a clear and concise manner. Remember, in all likelihood the web company works with dozens of businesses a year and knows little about your company and staff.

To clarify changes:
- Indicate where on a page you would like a change. "Remove the third paragraph on the "About" page and replace it with this text" or "Change 2012 to 2014 in the first paragraph of the History page."
- Be sure to be explicit regarding staff names. "Remove John Doe's bio and replace it with this text."
- Make sure you either name images clearly (ProductAJPG) or provide a key to indicate what the images are: "Jenny is in the green shirt, Trish is in the red."
- Be sure to indicate if something is being removed or replaced. "Remove the whole last paragraph, and replace it with these two sentences."
- Make sure to include all pertinent information, so your designer

won't have to contact you over and over. This includes new images, descriptions, prices, shipping rates and options for products.

- Of course, make sure all your changes are spelled correctly and are grammatically accurate, pictures are tagged accurately, prices are correct, etc. It is *your* job to provide the correct content, not the designer's to correct it.

Statistics

Modern web statistics are wonderful. John Wanamaker, a pioneer of advertising and marketing, once said, "Half the money I spend on advertising is wasted; the trouble is I don't know which half." With modern stats programs, you can get incredibly precise feedback on your website. You just need to take the time to look at it!

Statistics about visitors to your website include:
- How many people visited your website.
- How many were new visitors.
- Their geographical location.
- How long they stayed on the website.
- Which pages were viewed.
- How long they stayed on each page.
- The search terms they used to find your website.
- The search terms they used on your website.
- What months, days, and times visitors access your website.
- In what order visitors tend to navigate your website's pages.
- How many people abandoned their carts, and at what point in the checkout process.
- What browsers people used to access your website.
- What sort of computer/device people used to access your website.
- Load time (how fast the page loads for visitors).

Stats can help you understand your customers' needs and interests and also how to spend your advertising dollars. By knowing what parts of your website your visitors show the most interest in, you can get a good idea of what parts of your business they are looking for. Often a company will assume that products A and B are the main focus of their business, only to find a large portion of their audience looking for product C.

Website statistics can help you figure out:
- How people are finding your website, such as direct searches or being referred from other pages.
- Whether people are putting things in their carts. Do they abandon them at some point in the process, for instance, once they are notified of shipping rates? If so, can you make your shipping rates cheaper or more appealing in some way?
- What keywords people are using to get to your website. Are they pertinent? Do they relate to your company? Are they generic, or specific?
- Whether you get hits on landing pages created for online ads, Facebook posts or other targeted advertising. Or does most of your traffic still come through your homepage?
- Whether the numbers you see in your stats tally with what paid advertisers are telling, or promising, you?
- Whether visitors come back often, or only once.
- What path visitors take when they visit. For instance, do they come in on the homepage, then go to the sales page and then to the new products page?
- Where people leave the website. Seeing people leave from the contact page is always good news, but from an abandoned cart, not so much.
- Whether search terms appear that shouldn't, such as competitors' names or products.

- Whether there is higher traffic on certain days or at certain times.
- Whether there are other trends you can identify, such as seasonal trends.
- Where visitors are located. Do their locations agree with your customer lists or sales records?
- Whether you are getting a lot of hits from a country that makes no sense. If so, they may be trying to hack your website. Alert your host.

—

A friend of mine worked for a non-profit. Their staff was very proud of the fact that they got a lot of hits from what they assumed was name-recognition of their CEO. He was Thai, and his name was Mr. Thong (pronounced tong).

She never had the heart to tell them the truth.

—

At the very least, set up a Google Analytics account (google.com/analytics), Google Webmaster Tools (google.com/webmasters/tools) and the Bing toolbox (bing.com/toolbox/webmaster), which Yahoo! uses for their search terms. I am also quite fond of SiteMeter (sitemeter.com).

SEO

SEO, or search engine optimization, is one of those nebulous buzz-words that sounds so much less interesting and elegant when you describe it.

Essentially, SEO is:
- Making sure your website is up-to-date and accurate.

- Checking to make sure you have good content and descriptions.
- Resubmitting a website map and and URL to the search engines.
- Seeing what pops up in the various search engines when different terms are added.
- Reading any reviews about your company.
- Seeing who is linking to, or talking about your website.
- Reassessing what keywords and content should get the most emphasis.
- Updating contact and address information with online directories.

While you should take stock of how the website is functioning and make an effort every year or so to do the above updates, it isn't particularly scintillating or magical.

Rarely, if ever, do you need a company that specializes in "SEO optimization."

Be very, Very, VERY suspicious of any company that contacts you with promises about SEO (search engine optimization). Yes, maybe they *can* increase hits on your website. However, they don't promise an increase in *sales*. This is because many of these companies are scams. They send robots, computer programs, to ping your website for a millisecond. Are robots going to buy your products or use your services? Highly unlikely.

The same thing for "guaranteed ranking" on Google or other sites. Google itself warns there is no guarantee of top ranking, even if you are working through them with paid placement. An SEO company may be able to make you the number one search for "flying blue marmosets," but if you are a painter in Sheboygan, that doesn't really do you any good.

On the whole, if you need help with SEO, marketing and advertising, you should use the same rules you would use with hiring a web development company. *You* find *them*, look over their services, check out their other clients, see if there have been any complaints filed against them and get a quote. Also, find out if they offer any guarantees. If they do, they will be much more modest and realistic than the spam companies that send out mass emails.

Do Your Own SEO

You can also do your own mini-SEO now and again. I'd recommend doing the following at least once a year. This shouldn't take more than 2 hours.

To start off, search for your website by business name, plus a few combos of what you think your top keywords are. Be sure to use Google, Bing and Yahoo. What's your ranking (how close to the top of the first page are you)? If it isn't the top for your business name and location, you definitely need to do some work.

Take a look at the keywords your page shows up for. Are these the words you expected to show up for? Are you paying for any SEO or advertising where you choose keywords? Do they match they keywords that you are paying for?

Do you have odd terms that show up? For instance, I have tons of searches on my stats for "web design," "logo design" and other related terms. However, down at the bottom of the list are two searches for "paper mache snail." Seeing a few odd terms is pretty common. But if you see them a lot, your business may be categorized incorrectly somewhere, there is another business with a very similar name, or there may be some malicious code added to your website.

Check your search listing to make sure your address, phone and email are correct on your website and on any search listing. Send updates to any search engines that have incorrect information, particularly Google business listing. Don't have one? Set one up here: google.com/business.

Make sure your sitemap is updated. A sitemap is a file that lists all the pages in your website that you want search engine bots to read and categorize. Is the sitemap current? To create a new sitemap, go to a generator like xml-sitemaps.com. Once you snag the file, do make sure to read ti through to make sure there aren't any links you don't want listed. These may include administrative login pages or password protected areas. Most generators are very good at not listing these. Once you have a new sitemap, be sure to update it with Google, Bing and any other search engines you have registered an account with.

Look through your page titles. Are they descriptive? Far too often amateurs forget to add proper titles and will either have something generic like "home" or, even worse, the generic CMS titles welcoming them to a CMS-powered website. A title should describe the page, then the website. For instance, "Service Area Map: Joe's Emergency Plumbing, Sheboygan, WI."

Make sure you have either a good page description or that the first sentence or two of each page is highly descriptive. Google and other search engines have given up on reading the standard Meta tags (hidden keyword lists) due to "stuffing" (filling them with duplicate or unrelated words). They do however look at description tags. While you can no longer put in a bunch of hidden keywords saying "free beer" and expect people to come to your accounting site, you can give the website a good description. The first few lines of text on your site will show up in online searches, so make the sentence clear and descriptive. Instead of "Welcome, I'm so happy you're here. We love people! Hooray!" try "Welcome to West Side Optometry, located in the XYZ Mall, Sometown. We offer eye-care for all ages and specialize in bifocals for seniors."

If you blog or use the Posts feature in a WordPress site, make sure that your posts have clear categories and tags.

Check to make sure your images have "alt" tags on them, describing what they are. In particular, make sure products and people have a good alt tag, such as "Men's three-button henley shirt in forest green" rather than "green shirt." Often your products or images will get picked up by a search engine and put into either searches aimed directly at products, or into an image-only search area like Google's images.google.com.

Look through other sites that list your business. These include sites based on the old phonebook model, such as yellowpages.com, manta.com, yelp.com, superpages.com and others. There are dozens of other pages where you can acquire an account and a listing. I take these with a grain of salt. Many pull their listing information directly off Google or Yahoo!, so they may already have you listed (typos and all).

Check your location on Google Maps and MapQuest. Are you in the correct location and is your information displayed correctly?

Are you listed on any review sites like Angie's List, Urban Spoon or TripAdvisor? Is your information correct? Are there any reviews, positive or negative? If there are positive reviews, consider adding them to your website in a testimonials area. If they are negative, address both the reviewer and the problem as soon as possible (covered later).

Do you sell products through a third-party website like Amazon? Are there reviews? Are your product descriptions up-to-date, prices correct, images good? Is anything out of stock?

Are you listed on any professional, business association or club sites? Is your information up-to-date there? Is your website listed there? Do you link to them? Have any logos been updated?

Go to who.is and do a quick search on your website. When does your domain expire? Is that the correct phone and email on the account?

Is your business credit card set to expire (or expired!)? What needs to be updated: hosting, domain registry, third-party sites, PayPal, Google AdWords or Facebook Ads?

Pop over to browserstack.com and take a look at your website on some different browsers and devices. Does any part of the page look odd? If so, you may need to do some additional work on the appearance to accommodate new phones, tablets and browsers.

Put a few items in your cart, make a few changes on the amounts and shipping addresses, then go to the checkout. While this should have all been tested before the website launch, occasionally an update in a plugin or cart system can cause weird quirks. If you've noticed a drop-off in online sales, take this test all the way through checkout (you can refund yourself immediately afterwards) and try sending a few purchases through different browsers and devices.

Pull up any website analytics you have running and look through the entire year. What has changed? Has traffic steadily increased or decreased? Which pages have gotten more interest, which less? Have the traffic or demographic patterns changed? For instance, previously did you get people from New York City at 9 am on Monday morning, but now they tend to come at 4:30 pm on Friday? Why could this be? Do you have seasonal bumps? More hits during sales? Do these hits correspond to an actual increase in purchases?

If you are using a program like MailChimp for email newsletters, check out your statistics. How many new subscribers have you had? Did they sign up for certain lists? How many opted out? Why? What demographic(s) opened the emails and clicked through to your website? Which didn't?

Use your Google Analytics account and go to the Acquisition section, or to pages like wholinks2me.com to find out what sites are linking to you. Do you want to be associated with these sites? Do you see your website listed on their pages? Are they stealing your content, or just recommending you?

Unpleasant Reviews

While doing your research you may run across some unpleasant reviews, incorrect or misleading information or even other sites scraping (stealing) your content. There are varying degrees to which you can remedy these problems. If the problems are minor, such as incorrect contact information, this can usually be easily remedied by resubmitting your website and sitemap to the search engines and filling out update forms.

If the problem is a bad review and it is your fault, address it. If there isn't a way to directly contact the reviewer, do post a comment of your own with an apology and what you plan to do about it. However, if the review is libelous and you feel it can damage your brand, you may need to take legal action. In this case, you will need to contact either a lawyer or a reputation management company.

If content is being stolen or a company is misrepresenting itself as being in some sort of business relationship with your company, you will most likely need to send a cease and desist letter.

If you do need to consult with a lawyer, make sure you have as many pertinent facts as you can find.

What information you should try to include:

- Finding who the reviewer is, if possible. See if they have posted other negative reviews elsewhere. If they list a website, check out their registration via <u>who.is</u>.
- Take screenshots showing the review, in case they change or remove the content. While their host may be compelled to provide old back-ups in a court case, this is one of those "runs into money" scenarios.
- Use your website statistics or sales records to show whether the complaint has any validity. For instance, if a reviewer from Palo Alto, California writes a bad review, but you've never made a sale to that zip code, it may be a smear.
- Bring any correspondence that indicates that you tried to correct any negative complaints, and whether there was any response.

—

I had a client request I create a site just like his former business partner's—except cheaper, faster and smaller. He then threatened to sue me a few weeks later because his new business wasn't as big as his ex-partner's company.

—

Chapter 10
How Should I Advertise My Website?

Advertising on the web is both easier and more targeted than traditional print advertising. However, you must compete on a much larger scale (i.e., the world). In the early days of online advertising, you paid a flat fee for your ad placement, often without any say about what category it would show up in. Now you can choose the most granular of settings for your ad to be shown. This includes time, location, audience, related keywords and other even more finite settings. For instance, you can choose to have your ad showing 8-9 am, Monday - Friday to women ages 21-45 in San Francisco who use the terms "greenhouse," "garden center," or "landscaping" in their search terms or posts.

Google, Facebook and others let you set a budget for a period of time and how much you are willing to pay for each click. (A "click" is a visitor clicking on your website link, rather than just seeing your ad). So, you may set a budget of $100 for a month and offer $.25 for clicks on "greenhouse San Francisco" and $.45 for "greenhouse Noe Valley, San Francisco." The more specific and localized a search is, the more potential value it has to you as a business.

Excellent statistics reporting will give you clear feedback that print advertising never could offer. You may see that 200 people viewed your ad on Mondays, but only 3 people clicked. However, on Wednesdays, 150 viewed your ad and 15 people clicked on it. In the future, you may simply choose just to advertise on Wednesdays.

Targeted advertising allows you to choose specific keywords for set times with a set budget. They give you clear and direct feedback on who clicked, when they clicked, the viewer's location, how long they remained on the website and much more. The audience is limitless. You can reach anyone with access to the internet. Markets you didn't even know existed are now open to you. At the same time, you can target very specific audiences. There are a few drawbacks.

Often the most popular words are the most expensive. Focusing too much on only a small number of words can cause you to lose focus and ignore other words or areas that may also do well. While the audience is limitless, you are competing with companies all over the world, often with lower prices. Additionally, you may be neglecting other secondary audiences or ones you weren't even aware of. You need to be aware of the keywords you need to be targeting. What you *think* may be your target market may not really be the best group to be focused on.

What sort of keywords should you use, and where do you get them?
The vast majority of your keywords should be clear to you. They are the who, what, where, why and how of your business.

This includes:
- Your company name.
- Your location and service area (if applicable).
- Product names and descriptions.
- Services and descriptions.
- Permutations of names and products: "Milwaukee plumber," "plumbing Southeast WI," "emergency drain service, Third Ward, Milwaukee."
- Synonyms of products and services: "tax advisor," "accountant" or "CPA."

You don't want to waste money when choosing terms, nor do you want to have too many.
- **Be concise and descriptive with your terms.** "French business translation services" is far more accurate than "translation." It will also likely cost you less than the more generic keyword.

- **If your product or service is related directly to a location,** include it in the terms. "Viroqua Driftless Area WI campground" is far more specific than "campground." Someone going to the Driftless Region of Wisconsin to camp would be interested in your website. Someone going to camp in Kentucky, not so much. So why pay for the click when they in all likelihood won't be going to your location?
- Mention your target markets. "Women's steel-toed work boots" targets a much more specific group than "women's footwear."
- If you already have a stats program such as Google Analytics running on your website, you can see which pages and even which search terms people used to find you.
- Use any specific skills, brand names, products or other names that visitors may be familiar with. For instance, "specializing in Kohler plumbing design and installation" is far more specific than "plumbing installation."
- As with the website, be sure to provide a clean, clear and attractive picture of any product or logo that will go with the ad.

Email Lists

Setting up an email subscription list is a great way to stay in contact with customers. If you are already blogging or using social media, the same message can be trimmed and tailored for your email newsletters. Different users want to receive information in different ways, but that doesn't mean the content has to be totally different.

Many companies and groups have put out regular newsletters for years. Printing and mailing is costly. Transitioning to an email newsletter can save a great deal of money. Of course there are holdouts, and perhaps if the group is large enough you will need to continue doing the print newsletter. But it is well worth your while to look into adding email newsletters.

How Do I Create a List?

Use a company like MailChimp or Constant Contact to manage your list. This is one of the few times I suggest relying on a third-party for a service for your business. Both companies are free to start out, though they charge fees after you send a number of emails or your list grows to a certain size. These companies not only make it super-easy to join your list, but they also offer other terrific features, including:

- Opt-out links on emails, required by law under the CAN-SPAM Act.
- Code to allow sign-up through websites and social media.
- Easy uploads of existing email lists.
- Links that allow readers to share content with friends.
- The ability for users add themselves to different lists, based on interest.
- Easy-to-use templates that make your newsletter look beautiful and professional.
- Lots of options to sub-categorize users.
- Easy ways to embed images, links, videos and more.
- Terrific feedback on the number of people who opened the email, how many clicked through to your site, how many opted in or out (and why), where they are located, what time they opened your email and much more.
- The option to gather more than just a subscriber's email address, including name, address, phone number, interests and more.
- The ability to export your lists into a spreadsheet.

How Do I Get People to Sign Up?

We've all been burned by companies who have mercilessly spammed us. Getting people to part with their email is trickier than any other form of online marketing. With social media, you can easily unfollow or hide a feed you don't care about. With websites, you don't need to sign up or part with any information to read the content. Getting people to hand over their email requires trust, tact and persuasion.

The gray area on email lists consists of customers who have used your business, but have not explicitly agreed to be on your list. The safest bet is to add them to a list, then send them a welcome email, telling what the emails will contain and asking them if they'd like to receive future emails. Then make it clear that they can easily opt-out by clicking on a link. If they opt-out, you must, of course, honor that. But if the customers are happy with your service or product and interested in future discounts, coupons, news and more, they will most likely remain on the list.

If you want to be doubly sure about adding emails to your list, include some text on contact and registration forms and online checkouts. Offer people the option to opt-in (or opt-out) from your list then and there. Be sure to restate the benefits of joining and let them know they can leave at any time.

To get people to join your list, offer them something of value. Persuade them that signing up will benefit them in some way and state clearly why they are signing up. "Join our newsletter to get exclusive discounts," or "Join now to get our monthly tip. Available only to newsletter members."

Your email newsletters can contain the same information you have blogged or posted on social media. However, you can expand a bit more if you like, as you have a larger area to work with and a more captive audience.

To entice people to join your list:
- Offer discounts, coupons or specials that only available via the newsletter. *Be aware that some people will post those codes on places like retailmenot.com.*
- Send announcements to list members for goodies they can get

before the general public: sales, pre-orders, limited-edition or limited-time items, or events with a set number of tickets.

- Write articles related to your business, which can be virtually the same as your blog/news posts. Remember that different people have different preferences for getting their news. Some like an email, others an RSS feed, some like social media and still others like going directly to the website.
- Send short teasers about information that is available in full on the website. For instance, one of my clients posts a new recipe and cooking tip each month. Subscribers are reminded in the newsletter, but they need to go to the website to actually read them.
- Send information that **isn't** available anywhere else. For instance, only newsletter recipients get the recipe of the month.

NEVER send a newsletter to hundreds of contacts using your email address. That account will get blacklisted as a spammer.

If you are using a professional mailing company and have the emails formatted correctly (which MailChimp and Constant Contact will force you to do) then you shouldn't run into any issues with being blacklisted. People will sign themselves up and can take themselves off. Once someone has opted out of your list, you can't add them back on.

Don't Be a Jerk!

What does being a jerk entail? The biggies are:

- Sending too many emails.
- Not having an opt-out mechanism.
- Not honoring opt-outs.

- Sharing or selling your contact list.
- Adding people who have not done business with your company without their permission.

Buying email lists or signing up random emails is a really bad idea. Beyond the obvious "it's illegal and really rude" arguments, you can hurt your own brand. Do you want to be known for your products and services, or for sending tons of spam? Don't forget, there are plenty of places people can review your company and make their complaints known. There are also official channels where they can file complaints about you.

Also, why waste time and money pestering people who have no interest in your product or service? If they are on your list and leave, no harm, no foul. They are no longer interested. Or, perhaps they would prefer to get their information about your brand elsewhere. If you have your email list going through a company like MailChimp, you are able to ask people why they are opting out. You may find that people simply would rather hear about you in their Facebook feed or through Twitter.

Be warned, if you do send thousands of emails out to people who then opt out (citing you as spam), your email newsletter account can be blocked or shut down.

—

The contact lens brand I use sends an email every single day even though I have repeatedly opted-out and marked them as spam. I buy contacts once a year and I've seriously considered switching brands just because they irritate me so much.

—

Print Is Not Dead!

While the web has definitely given print a run for its money, print is most certainly NOT dead. The two now work in tandem; you cannot rely on only one or the other to get your message out. However, with a good website, you won't need to spend nearly as much on print advertising. Instead, you can have smaller ads with less content that send your customers to your website for full product listing and services.

So, where should you have your web address, email and social media sites listed?
- In any print ads you run – newspaper, magazines, yellow pages.
- On business cards, letterhead, brochures, postcards, receipts, catalogs and other company materials.
- On company vehicles.
- In any business listings you may have, such as the Chamber of Commerce, social or business club listings, sponsorship listings or donor listing.
- In any on-air advertising – radio and TV ads, NPR and PBS sponsorship, interviews.
- In any articles, op-eds, or commentaries submitted for print.
- When commenting online on professional forums or message boards.

Chapter 11

Should You Use Social Media?

Social media like Facebook, Twitter, LinkedIn, Pinterest and other sites can be a great help or a massive time-waster. Be realistic about how much time you spend on them and determine whether you get any positive, tangible feedback from them. If business and sales increase, they are working. If not, consider what you can do differently. Or, just stop spending so much time on them.

If using social media regularly doesn't increase sales, spend that time on a different aspect of promotion.

Social media is free to use. It is quick and easy to post and you can reach thousands, and potentially even millions of people. Social media can help you reach all sorts of markets and audience groups. It can provide response from a vast array of demographics and market segments. Many social media sites allow anyone to access your information, so you don't need to go to the trouble of finding interested readers.

However, while these services don't cost anything monetarily (unless you pay for advertising) they can cost you a great deal of time that could be spent on other endeavors. The ease with which you can post can cause you to type hastily, spell poorly and write ungrammatically. This makes you look uneducated and unprofessional. Reducing your message to a mere snippet can also dilute and reduce the message's power. Simply because you can reach people, doesn't mean they are paying attention (or care). Any website that allows public comment is opening itself up for abuse from spammers, trolls and other nasty people. Be prepared to deal with this.

Have you ever walked into a mall at Christmas and been hit with a tsunami of "BUY! BUY! BUY!"? It's overwhelming, isn't it? Followers of your social media feeds or blog will feel the same if all you post is about purchasing your products or services. Overwhelm your visitors with continual demands that they buy your products and they will probably react the way I do in a Christmas-encrusted hell–leave or turn on the blinders. Your followers will soon grow tired of the continual cajoling to buy and remove themselves from the feeds or lists. Or they will tune you out until they see specific key word, like "coupon" or "yearly sale." You want to increase sales, not alienate and irritate customers.

Some Basic Dos and Don'ts for Social Media:

- Do encourage people to take action from your posts. For instance, buy something, sign up for a list, share with a friend. Make sure this action is clear and easy to perform.

- Don't bore your audience. Simply stating over and over again that you have products to sell is tedious, and you will soon lose any followers you may have. Think of a small child shouting "Look at me! Look again! Lookit!" Change up the message regularly.

- Do provide something of worth in your posts. In return, customers will become loyal to your product or service. These items may include sales, advice, interesting links or other tangentially related information.

- Do make it all about you. If you are writing a blog post on something tangentially related to your business, remember to bring it around to your product or service...tastefully. For instance, if you are an author and are using some research you did on Victorian shoes to create a blog post, do remember to mention that your heroine wears shoes like these in your new book, available from Amazon (click here!).

- Do name drop, as long as it is not obnoxious. For instance, your travel agency may specialize in tours of England in the counties where Midsomer Murders is filmed. You aren't actually tied to the show, but those interested in England, travel and the program would be likely to be interested in your services.

- Do list quality brand names. Many people are loyal to certain companies and by offering them, you also acquire some of the "glow." Without even realizing it, many people use brand names instead of the actual product's name. For instance, we often say "Kleenex" instead of "tissue."

- Do post regularly. This doesn't mean you have to do it every day, let alone hourly. Your audience will be much more appreciative of one quality post a week rather than daily blather.

- Do use programs like HootSuite or Twuffer to set up posts to submit themselves for upcoming blocks of time, perhaps during a busy season or when you will be on vacation.

- Do make sure all posts or tweets are approved by you or a responsible member of your staff. Too often social media is off-loaded to an intern or lower-level staff member. They may not have the best judgement on what the company message should be (as many large companies have found to their embarrassment). Remember, what appears on the net stays on the net.

- Don't focus on your existing friends and followers, particularly personal friends. They already know a great deal about you and your company and don't need to be reminded. Increase your audience. Tailor your messages towards new visitors and potential customers. Use interesting, informative tidbits to draw in new users, then be sure there are ways for their interest to be turned to profit.

- Don't waste a lot of time on social media if it isn't working. There is definitely the mental lure of, "Well, it's free to use." But your time isn't. If your posts don't cause an increase in tangible sales or other actions you desire, then they are merely eating into time you could be promoting your business in another way. Or posting cat videos for your friends.

What are some things you can include to make your posts interesting and worth following?
- Tips related to your service/product, such as repairs, set-up and different uses.
- Interesting historical notes.
- Quotes.
- Fun Facts.
- Interesting and cool links to related articles.
- Coupon codes.
- Flash sale announcements.
- Invitations to events.
- Praise for your employees, a local charity you support, good customer service, etc.
- Testimonials or good reviews.
- Asking questions of followers to increase engagement. "Do you like it when stores decorate before Thanksgiving? Why or why not?"

Which of these media sites should you use?
- **Twitter:** Allows you to post 140 character "tweets" with keywords set apart by hashtags (pound signs). You can set your account so that anyone can read your tweets, creating a very wide audience. For instance "Two for one #shoesale, today only at #ourshop #ourtown." Tweets can be "re-tweeted," pre-set to post automatically, and can include links (such as a link to your online shoe sale page) and pictures and videos. Use Twitter for short blasts of information that then guide visitors back to your website.
- **Facebook:** Allows you to compose longer posts. You can include

images and links which encourage readers to make comments and share your posts. You may also create photo albums, linked advertising and more. One drawback is that Facebook often tinkers with rankings and what and how posts appear in peoples' feeds.

- **LinkedIn:** Tailored for professionals seeking business contacts, this website may be ideal if you are looking to network and build business-to-business relationships. LinkedIn lets you promote yourself with a resume, information on past and present jobs, business relationships and more. However, it doesn't have the fun immediacy of Facebook or Twitter.
- **Instagram/Pinterest/Houzz/Kaboodle/Polyvore/Tumblr:** There are many sites that allow you to post images, projects and ideas. You can pin or suggest your products on these sites.

How Do I Sign Up?

All of these sites will have clear sign-up procedures. Do make sure to indicate that you are signing up for a business account, rather than a personal one. Bear in mind as you post that this is a business account. Try not to let the lines blur and start posting personal information on your business account. This includes personal commentary on politics, religion, personal health and relationships, financial information, rants/complaints/manifestos or links that are not directly or tangentially related (i.e. no cat videos, unless you are a vet or pet store). And, of course, nothing illegal or unethical.

Some of these sites will require contact information for your business. If you want to use them, you may have to provide a phone number, email and street address. This is an excellent reason to have a business phone line, business email account and, if you are a home business, a PO Box. You may not notice a huge up-tick in spam or telemarketing calls, but it will increase to some degree regardless. If you post it, they will find it.

I had a client ask me to include Facebook and Twitter icons on their website. I asked for the feed addresses and was told, "We don't actually have any accounts, we just want to show people we are aware of social media."

Oh.

Never Rely Solely on Third-Party Social Media

There are a number of reasons you *should not* rely on social media as your only web presence. Here's why:

- **Free products do not always remain free.** If you build your web presence solely on a free third-party platform and they then start charging, you are either forced to pay what they ask or lose your data. Unlike building a website, you won't have any up-front knowledge of what this cost will be. If you can't or won't pay the fee, your web presence goes away.

- **You owe them everything, they owe you nothing.** For the most part, these companies make their money mining your data to sell to advertisers. One user is negligible to them, so there is virtually **no support** for when things go wrong.

- While there is always a chance that the security on your website may be breached, you are generally told in third-party sites' sign-up pages that **you can't expect any privacy when using their sites**. They will mine your information and sell it to advertisers. They may use your pictures, quote you, tie your profile to other products or companies and more. If you don't want your brand muddied, especially without your permission or knowledge, keep most of your content in a website that you own and control.

- **Third-party companies can and do go belly up.** If you have all of your content at a third-party website and they go out of business, you may never get any of it back. Suddenly your web presence is gone, and there is no one to contact.

- **Your account can be removed for no reason.** If someone lodges a false complaint, you post something that the company does not approve of or there is simply a technical glitch, your account and content can be removed. Because you have no contract and have not made any payments to them, there is little to no recourse in getting the account back. Again, there is almost no technical support from these companies and you have no leverage with which to threaten them.

Chapter 12
What Happens When It Breaks?!

"Have you tried turning it off and on again?" - The IT Crowd

Sorry, but stuff happens. Sites go down, email bounces back, spammers attack, you lose your network connection, someone hacks your account...

There are a few things you should always try before contacting tech support for help:

- Refreshing your browser.
- Restarting your browser or computer.
- Seeing whether you can access other sites.
- Checking the website on another device.
- **Reading** any error warnings.

Usually these will solve or explain 90% of your issues.

ALWAYS know who to contact BEFORE it breaks.

Knowing who to contact and how to describe your problem is essential to getting your website or email up and running again. Calling your web developer or host's tech support and saying "It's not working" is about as useful as going to your doctor and saying "Something hurts." Your doctor would ask you a slew of questions, which then would allow him or her to perform diagnostics and tests to determine the problem and find a solution.

Provide as many details up-front as you can. This includes:

- Your operating system, the big three being Windows, Macintosh and Linux.
- Your operating system version number and name. For instance,

Windows XP or OSX Mountain Lion. Not sure? On a Mac, go to the desktop, then click on the apple icon at the top left corner. Go to About This Mac. On Windows, go to <u>whatsmyos.com</u> for directions.

- If you are having problems with a website, find out which browser you are using. The browser is the program you use to view websites. You are probably using Firefox, Google Chrome, Safari, Opera or Internet Explorer.
- Once you are in your browser, go to the main menu and find "About [your browser name]" to get the version information. This will probably be a number, such as Google Chrome Version 38.0.2125.111.
- Describe what you tried to do and what happened. For instance, "I tried to go to my website and the screen is white. The loader icon just keeps twirling." Or, "There is nothing on my website but this database error message [include message]."
- Describe any error messages on the website or pop-up warnings you are getting. If possible, get them word-for-word.
- Describe any other actions you tried. For instance, did you refresh or restart the browser, did other pages work, did the website work on your phone but not your desktop machine? Experiment a bit to try to narrow the problem.

Once you have the problem nailed down, you should be able to describe it very succinctly. "I'm on a Mac Powerbook running Maverick and using Google Chrome Version 38.0.2125.111. I tried to access my website at 9:30 am. First it loaded a blank page for about 20 seconds. Once I refreshed, it gave me this message: 'Database Error: Unable to connect to the database: Could not connect to MySQL.' It didn't work on my iPhone either and it still isn't loading."

Even if this is all gibberish to you, it will help the tech support a great deal. Additionally, **contact the tech support** as soon as possible. It is MUCH easier to nail down a problem while it is happening than hours later, when it has often resolved.

Who Do You Contact?

If the website isn't loading (but other sites do) or there is a database error: Contact the host directly. If you are using a design company you can contact them, but they will typically relay your problem to the host. This just adds an additional, unneeded step. Provide all the details you can on the problem, the full and correct web address, the time it happened, your name and contact information and whether it has resolved or not.

Many hosts will require you to log in to a control panel to submit a support ticket. Make sure you know your control panel login information or the email address for direct support. You may also need to provide proof of ownership. This may include: FTP passwords, the email or phone number used to register the domain or set up hosting, the last four digits of a credit card used to register the website or phrases/words that were chosen when the website was set up. Either have this information on hand, or have the person who set them up take care of contacting support.

You may also want to call tech support. Ideally, you should try to find a direct support line rather than a general business line. It really depends on the hosting company on which form of contact will get you faster help. For instance, my favorite host, northtone.com, has terrific, fast email support. Godaddy has abysmal email support but great phone support. I have yet to get any sort of useful support via any live chat programs. Usually the best you can get with chat is to request a direct tech support number.

If the website is fine, but you are getting an password error: a few things may have happened. There may have been an attack on the website or a security breach. In this case, the host often changes access passwords. They *should* let you know that the password has been changed, but there are a few companies that are notoriously bad about not doing this. You could have forgotten the password. Or someone could have gotten access to your account and changed it.

If the error is with **FTP access**, then you need to either go into your control panel and reset the FTP password or contact the host's tech support.

If the error is with your **control panel**, you will either need to request a password reset (there is usually a link) or contact tech support.

If the error is **with an account**, you may need to request a password reset. Most login pages will have a password reset link. The reset password will be sent to the email with which you registered the account.

If you are informed that there is **no account** attached to that email, you will have to contact your host's tech support, as your account has been deleted or you are using the wrong email.

If there is an access or IP blocked error: then the IP (internet protocol) address from which you are attempting to view the website has been blacklisted. You will need to contact your Internet Service Provider (ISP). This is your internet service company. The biggest are Time/Warner, AT&T, Verizon, ComCast, Charter, and CenturyLink. To verify the account ownership, tech support may request personal information, such as the last four digits of a credit card. Sometimes this problem can be resolved, though it is often very tricky. Usually it is easier for them to assign you a new IP.

If your domain has expired or you have unpaid bills: your website may be taken down. Usually these problems are just issues with expired credit cards or outdated emails, which is why there is a grace period. There will generally be a message on your domain for about 30-45 days detailing what to do. You may be instructed to update your credit card with your host or domain registry. Beyond that grace period, your domain will start showing a notice that it is available for purchase. The host will most likely delete your files and email accounts after 45 days (maximum).

If you haven't paid for work done by a web development company, they may freeze or remove your website. Refer to your contract to see what terms of payment and arbitration are required. If you've simply chosen not to pay, don't expect a lot of sympathy... or to see your website or emails again.

If nothing is loading or you cannot connect to the internet: then you need to contact your Internet Service Provider (AT&T, Verizon, ComCast, etc.). In all likelihood, you won't be able to email (because internet is down, see) so you will need to call tech support. This is a time when having a direct phone number for support is a great help.

Browser, Device and Platform Compatibility

There are very real differences between the way a website functions on different platforms, browsers, versions and devices. What looks wonderful on one can have some bizarre problems on another. (For an idea of how different sites can work and function, pop over to browserstack.com and put in a website address, then choose some different device options to compare.)

As of April 2015, Google has started removing sites from its mobile search engines that are not mobile-friendly, based on their standards. Check your website's compatibility here:

google.com/webmasters/tools/mobile-friendly/
Most push-button programs have these bugs ironed out (primarily because there aren't that many options for you to use). But if you are making the website yourself, you must be aware of this. The awesome website you put together in Dreamweaver may look great on your huge, high-resolution monitor. However, it may be almost unusable on your phone. You can't just create a website for desktop/laptop monitors any more. You must also be prepared to make the website work cross-browser/cross-platform/cross-device.

A note about Internet Explorer (IE): Web professionals hate IE. Really, it's up there with the Comic Sans font as things we loathe. There are international standards set on how a browser should work set by a group called W3C (World Wide Web Consortium). Most browser makers follow these standards... except for IE. IE has its own "standards," which by this definition, are not at all standard. They are often a few steps behind all the other browsers for functionality. Most sites need at least a little, and often A LOT of additional code tweaking to work well on IE. In fact, some design companies are now charging extra to make sites compatible in IE, and others are simply refusing to allow IE users to access their pages.

Why do people use it? Users don't know any better. It is free and comes with their Windows PC. While it is being phased out, many many people still have it installed.

Do yourself a favor. If you don't *have* to use IE, download a different browser. They are free and you'll be shocked what a better web viewing experience you will have. If you have to use IE or insist on having a website that is totally compatible with IE, expect to pay a small to large chunk of change to have it be as functional as it would be on other browsers.

Chapter 13
What Web Security Do You Need?

Nothing is ever really gone on the web. Ever. Ever. Ever. If you don't want people finding it, don't put it on the internet or email it. Period. Ever.

While it may seem obvious that you need to have security to process credit cards, other forms of web security may be surprising.

These are the big no-nos:
- Email is not at all secure. Don't ever request that sensitive personal information be sent via email. This includes: social security numbers, credit card numbers, bank account numbers, medical records, birth date or other details that could not be found via public record or simple search engine searches.
- Don't ask for information that it is illegal to request. For instance, posting a job application and asking for race, gender, nationality, religion, military status, age, etc. If it is illegal to ask for in person, don't ask for it on a form.
- Keep sensitive information, such as classified documents or legal files, off the internet and out of your email. If you don't have a secure system in place to transfer these files, use snail mail.

Most of the big no-nos are pretty commonsense. But you can often get yourself into just as much trouble with other content.

Think twice or get approval before posting:
- Personal contact information or photos of staff.
- Content that is intended for internal use only. If you need to share

files with staff online, consider building an intranet. Otherwise, double-check to make sure these files are password protected and that the web pages have no-follow code so search engine robots don't add them to their indices.

- Wholesale pricing or any special pricing for which only certain merchants are eligible.

- Comments on an employee's status (current or otherwise), unless it is positive. If you must say something about a terminated, former or deceased employee, keep it factual and as minimal as possible. It's not your place to reveal why someone was fired, why they left or how they died.

- Linking to companies or sites that you haven't done business with or hired yourself. By recommending another company, you are tying yourself to them and their performance. However, if they have done an excellent job for you, do go ahead and recommend them. For instance, "Come see our new reception area and floor-to-ceiling windows, installed by XYZ company."

- Don't imply an association that you don't have. For instance, you may be a woman-owned business, but that doesn't give you the right to put a Small Business Administration "Women Owned Small Business Certified" logo on your page unless you've filled out the paperwork and been approved.

Conclusion

Hopefully what needs to be done to create a website is now clear and you have a better understanding of what goes into creating a website. As you can see, there are many, often complex, parts to creating a website. However, by planning your site, you can save yourself an immense amount of time and hassle. Maybe you had planned to create the website yourself, but realized that you simply don't have the skill and need to hire someone else. Or perhaps you've decided that your budget doesn't extend to a web development company now, so it's time to take a few evening classes on creating a simple website. Whatever you decide, it should be the right thing for *your* business. Good luck!

The Author

Elaine Meszaros started designing websites back in the day when they could only have 256 colors and had to be hand-coded in HTML, uphill both ways, *in a snowstorm,* **with wolves nipping at her heels!** Elaine's clients include authors, artists, manufacturers, unions, retail shops, therapists, speakers and everyone in-between. 99% of her clients are lovely, organized people who pay their bills on time and would never *dream* of asking her to reschedule her honeymoon for a meeting.

The other 1% provided the anecdotes for this book.